1 MONTH OF
FREE
READING

at
www.ForgottenBooks.com

By purchasing this book you are eligible for one month membership to ForgottenBooks.com, giving you unlimited access to our entire collection of over 1,000,000 titles via our web site and mobile apps.

To claim your free month visit:
www.forgottenbooks.com/free75105

ISBN 978-1-5280-6844-4
PIBN 10075105

BOERS

AND

LITTLE ENGLANDERS

The Story of

the Conventions

By JOHN PROCTER

BARRISTER-AT-LAW

LONDON
GEORGE ALLEN, 156 CHARING CROSS ROAD
1897

Printed by BALLANTYNE, HANSON & Co.
At the Ballantyne Press

INTRODUCTION

THE chief object of this book is to render the position of Her Majesty as Suzerain over the South African Republic intelligible to all.

Few persons seem to be aware that Her authority as paramount Power is derived from the Convention of Pretoria of 1881, and not from the London Convention of 1884.

The former Convention is still in full force in so far as the Queen's guarantee and Suzerain rights are concerned, and the 1884 Convention is only supplemental and ancillary to it. The latter deals solely with the substitution of Articles for those of the former Convention, and it in no way alters the declaration made in 1881.

It will be found that the story of the Transvaal has been told in chronological order, from the trek in 1836 down to the present day; and almost all the facts set forth, save what have come under my personal observation whilst in South Africa, are corroborated by evidence from Blue Books placed from time to time before Parliament.

Thus I have dealt :

(1) With the manner in which the South African Republic sprang into existence.

(2) With the annexation by us of that country in 1877, and the incidents which compelled us to that step.

(3) With the events prior to the Convention of 1881.

(4) With the Convention itself.

(5) With what transpired after the ratification of the Convention, and the surrender in 1884 by Mr. Gladstone's Cabinet of its most important provisions.

(6) With the situation to-day.

I have felt it my duty from my own personal experience of the brutal treatment of Kaffirs by Boer officials, in open violation of Article 19 of the Convention of 1884, to devote a chapter specially to this subject.

Outrages on the persons and property of natives, as well as murders in cold blood, have reached such proportions as to rouse the indignation of every British man and woman ; and, for the honour of England, it is to be hoped that Her Majesty's Government will peremptorily demand that this portion of the Convention be strictly observed.

I have further introduced a chapter on the Hollander,

which I regard as very necessary, when we consider the enormous influence now exercised by this group of foreigners over the Boer Executive and Government.

My work has no pretensions to literary merit. It is a plain, unvarnished tale, and the information thus collected will, I trust, be found useful to the great masses of those, both at home and abroad, who have interests in South Africa. If, perchance, its perusal should incite the members of the Parliamentary Committee, now sitting, to make inquiries as to the guarantee and obligations undertaken in 1881 towards the inhabitants of the Transvaal State in the name of Her Majesty, and should further induce them to take a firm stand, I shall feel I have not laboured in vain. I have added an Appendix (including the texts of the Conventions of 1881 and 1884), in which will be found copies of several documents corroborative of my views.

J. P.

May 22, 1897.

CONTENTS

Boers and Little Englanders

CHAPTER I

ORIGIN OF THE SOUTH AFRICAN REPUBLIC

About the year 1835 the descendants of the Dutch and
Huguenot families settled at the Cape were roused to a
pitch of deadly resentment against British rule.   Ever
since the beginning of the century, when the Dutch
possessions in Africa were ceded to England, relations
between the British military authorities and the
"Boers" (as these Dutch settlers were called) had
been more than strained and, as the years rolled on,
these Boers openly resented our masterful power over
them, and compared it to the tyranny exhibited towards
their fathers by their own Dutch East India Company
of a generation earlier.

The climax was reached when England proclaimed
the total abolition of slavery in the country.   Our
Government promised to compensate the masters
liberally for the losses incurred by the enforced
emancipation of their slaves, and were lavish in their
assurances that sums of money would be handed over

A

to the farmers to cover the expense of hired labour. But, in the main, these promises were unfulfilled, and scarce a tenth part of the funds agreed upon ever reached the farmer's hands.

What followed is a story tragic in the extreme, and one of the most pathetic in the history of the century.

Ruined in pocket, their hearts filled with bitter hatred towards the Government which had played them false, and without the power of fighting for their own interests, they deserted the homes they could no longer keep, and wandered with their families northward and eastward, trying to find in the wilderness of the Veldt a resting-place, where at least they would be free from hated foreign official interference. Here they had ample time to brood over their wrongs. Cut off from the outside world, they had but their own misfortunes and the incidents of their daily life as food for reflection. Their only literature was the Bible, and in its perusal the strong and deeply religious tendency inherited from their forefathers daily gained force, until they began to interpret the Old Testament histories as referring to themselves, and to identify their mode of existence with that of the Israelites. Indeed, in their appalling ignorance so fully did they become imbued with the belief that they were a suffering people selected by God to work out their own salvation, that by a very simple process of analogy they were further convinced that they were the descendants of the Patriarchs, and as such were bound to accept the Old Testament as their guide and to live in accord with its injunctions.

These Boers were grim obstinate folk, both men and women, for the latter shared all dangers, and though a woman personally did not carry a gun she could load and fire one when needed, at times a most helpful accomplishment. Their religion was entirely of the militant order, the New Testament being to them practically a sealed book and no doctrine of peace or mercy ever entering into their theology.

At this period each family dwelt in a rudely constructed waggon drawn by oxen. They kept together for safety's sake, drawing up their waggons at night so as to form a temporary fortress against possible foes. Around the camp fires old and young assembled. Conversation amongst the elders was limited to the incidents of the day and to discussions on passages culled from their one book, from which they likened their own wanderings to those of the children of Israel. Fortified in this belief, they taught the younger generation that every black was the born bondsman of the white, and, moreover, that they were the chosen instruments appointed by divine command to be the black man's master, and to take possession of his lands as their natural heritage. It must not be supposed that everything went smoothly in their different communities or that all agreed, even on the interpretation of the Scriptures. On the contrary, the want of diversion in their lives and the close neighbourhood of persons who had previously dwelt at long distances from one another naturally brought about divisions of opinion and even dissensions.

On two points they were, however, united. First, hostility towards the Englishman; and secondly, subjugation of the Kaffir; and on these their energies were invariably concentrated.

It is well known that impressions of early youth exercise a powerful influence over men's future lives, especially when such impressions are graven on the memory by the solemnity of events in which they personally take part.

Now, a leading characteristic of the youthful Boer always has been a strong respect, amounting even to reverence, for the views and opinions of his elders.

No wonder then that he who had joined in the difficulties and adventures of his father determined in his turn to pursue the dominant idea, and go forth into the world to establish a home. Limited though his education, his wits were sharpened by the conflicting adversities of his daily life, and in Dame Nature's school he soon acquired a knowledge of character far wider and more profound than is ordinarily possessed by a member of more civilised communities.

Amongst the young Boers there was no more apt pupil than Stephanus Johannis Paulus Kruger. Keen, shrewd and valorous, endowed with a strong physique, doggedly obstinate, and steeped in the history of Moses and Joshua, he soon became marked by his elders as one to be admitted to their deliberations. But, withal, he vigorously maintained his independence of party and never allied himself to any faction which was not prepared to pursue the path or policy which he had decided in his own mind ought to be followed.

The Boer modified his fighting tactics by the lessons of personal experience taught him in his frequent conflicts with his native foes. Soon his expertness in forming "laager," or in taking advantage of every bush or ant-hill calculated to afford protection against his enemy's bullet or assegai, as well as his own sure aim, won him reputation as a formidable antagonist.

Ever on the move, and constant in his determination to acquire land, although his knowledge of agriculture has never ceased to be of the most primitive character, it is not at all surprising that the population became scattered sparsely over a very large area as the years went by.

Within fifteen years of the exodus of 1835, different groups of these wanderers had spread over what are now the Orange Free State and the British Colony of Natal, whilst others had established themselves to the north of the Vaal River, many powerful Kaffir tribes having been subdued in the meantime. At first, and indeed for some years, these farmers beyond the Vaal obeyed the military and civil authority of tried and accepted leaders. In course of time, however, dissensions arose between different commanders, and serious bickerings broke out on religious matters to such an alarming extent that the more enlightened amongst them determined to create a form of government directly representative of the people's will. Hence we find that in the year 1849 a Volksraad or parliament was instituted to which delegates were elected by popular vote. Meanwhile, the Imperial policy of England towards her Colonies had undergone those great changes which ultimately led to the establishment of a Colonial Department of the Home Government as distinguished from the control hitherto of the War Office. In 1852, after many disputes with the English authorities at the Cape, an arrangement known as the Sand River Convention was arrived at between Her

Majesty and those Boers who had crossed the Vaal (at whose head were two sagacious and valiant men named Andries Pretorius and Piet Potgieter), wherein the Boers were granted self-government under certain defined conditions, and were recognised as a nation under the title of the South African Republic. To achieve this result they had conquered Kaffir hordes in many a stubborn fight, and, possessing the blind belief that they were God's messengers to do His work, it is not strange that they looked on the soil and the natives as a direct gift to them from the Almighty. No assistance had been rendered them by any other race during those long years of trial. They and they alone had made almost superhuman sacrifices, had endured untold privations, and had freely shed their blood to accomplish this object—a home and country free from foreign interference.

Is it singular, then, that in their hearts they should claim for themselves the sole right of representation in the Government of the State, to the exclusion of every other settler ?

In order to grasp the situation fully, we must consider the narrow limits of their social intercourse, confined for years to peripatetic meetings with other wandering religious fanatics of their own race, their intermarriages, and their moral and intellectual training. It will then be understood how these slow-thinking, ignorant and suspicious farmers felt (and still feel) that every promise they made, whether oral or written, which might have the effect of placing outsiders on an equality with them, had been extorted by superior force, and was not, therefore, binding on their conscience.

Most essential is it to understand this curious moral attitude ere we pass judgment on their flagrant disregard of all pledges, and open violation of all compacts. Let us be clear on this point. Whenever the terms and conditions expressed in Articles of different Conventions appear inimical to their interests, these Boers have never considered themselves bound to respect them, and this has been their line of action from the early days of the Sand River Convention down to the present year of grace. Once the right to govern themselves had been granted by Her Majesty in 1852, and before the Convention was ratified by their lately constituted Volksraad, a serious quarrel broke out between their two chief commanders, Potgieter and Pretorius, who were each supported by a body of adherents. And here Paul Kruger played an important part. Sometimes with Potgieter, and at others against him, but always acting as a sort of firebrand amid the factions, he took the line that the Zoutpansberg and Lydenburg Boers should be welded into the South African Republic.

The matter became at one time so grave as to render a civil war imminent, but the strong common sense of the two principals prevailed; they became reconciled, and the dark cloud passed. Attention was then directed towards the framing of a Constitution, and after repeated meetings in different parts of the Republic, and many disagreements over details, this was finally accomplished in 1858. This Constitution, based more or less on that of the United States of America, was solemnly accepted by the people, and is now recognised as their charter under the name of

"Grondwet." All functions appertaining to Government, including the administration of justice, were usually carried out by those more enlightened and cultivated descendants of the old Dutch and Huguenot stock from the Cape Colony and Orange Free State, of whose services the more ignorant among the Transvaal Boers gladly availed themselves. But in a community such as this, the duties of judges and magistrates were obviously not very heavy. Financial affairs, however, were more serious, and as the difficulty of finding money for ordinary State purposes asserted itself, it will be readily understood that a revenue officer stood a very poor chance of collecting taxes from these wandering nomads.

As the young Republic grew in years, it became ever increasingly difficult for the authorities to raise money sufficient even for necessary defensive requirements. Strife had broken out amongst the Boers on the everlasting religious and territorial questions. In consequence, they became jealous and mistrustful of each other, until at last their condition was such that towards the close of 1876 they were not merely bankrupt as a nation, but had become totally unfitted for self-government.

From the uncompromising character of the man and with our knowledge of his narrow, bigoted, religious views, it is not singular that in that year we find Paul Kruger had attained to the position of a member of the Executive, and Vice-President of the Republic, the head of the State being a quiet cultured man, President Thomas Burgers. Neither is it surprising, when we consider the training and mode of life of the two men, that on all matters of expediency relating to the Government or the future destinies of the Republic, their views were as wide apart as the poles. The more educated of the community supported the President, but the Voortrekkers either stood aloof or trusted to Kruger, who urged them to continue the struggle for the maintenance of their independence, although he was incapable of suggesting a way out of the difficulty which their own dissensions and incapacity had brought about.

CHAPTER II

ANNEXATION BY ENGLAND

WITH their usual aggressiveness towards natives, the Boer Government in the year 1876 seized lands belonging to an independent Kaffir chief named Sekukuni, who, though by no means powerful in comparison with others on their borders, utterly routed the Boer forces. In short, the Boers displayed such cowardice in their attack on Sekukuni's stronghold that their President Thomas Burgers had to raise a force of mercenaries regardless of nationality, by the offer to each of £5 per month and a farm at the end of the campaign. This body was commanded by a German, named Von Schlickman. Matters progressed from bad to worse, and other native chiefs, emboldened by Sekukuni's success, began to threaten both the Boers and our own colonists. Notable among these was the Zulu King Cetewayo, the most powerful of all, who in haughty terms declared his intention to "allow his young men to wash their spears."

Sir Henry Barkly, at that time Governor of Cape Colony, in a letter dated October 30, 1876, to the Earl of Carnarvon, Secretary of State for the Colonies, explanatory of the situation, expressed himself as follows* :—

"5. Thirteen volunteers it is further stated had reached Pretoria from the Diamond Fields, sixty or seventy more being expected the week after, and Von Schlickman had gone on before them to Lydenburg, to the military command of which district he has been officially gazetted.

"6. He is said likewise to have been appointed by President Burgers to collect the taxes there with a salary of £1 a day and 5 per cent. on the amount collected.

"7. This appointment, as your Lordship will perceive from the enclosed letter, which has just reached me from the chairman of the Defence Committee at Pilgrims Rest, has excited much apprehension, in consequence of Von Schlickman having recommended when examined before the Volksraad 'that the Gold Fields should be subdued.'

"8. It is feared that an attempt to coerce the diggers into exorbitant payments by armed force will be made, the impression that this is contemplated acquiring strength from the summary suppression of the office of Special Magistrate, which is described in the letter as an arbitrary and unconstitutional act.

"9. Nor is the discontent confined to the Gold Fields population only. At a public meeting held in Lydenburg on the 2nd inst., before the appointment of Von Schlickman was known, resolutions moved by some of the oldest and most influential inhabitants of Dutch

* See Blue Book C 1748, No 148, p. 178.

extraction were unanimously carried, condemning the continuance of the war and the imposition of war taxes, and in favour of Confederation and of applying for British intervention in the dispute with Sekukuni.

" 10. I append a translation of the petition to the President and the Volksraad founded thereon, which is said to have been signed by nearly every adult male inhabitant of Lydenburg and Kruger's Post.

" 11. As the Volkraad had been prorogued before it reached Pretoria, this expression of opinion could have little effect, and it has since been determined in default to open negotiations with Sekukuni, at whose mercy for weeks past the district has virtually lain, the Boers from a distance commandeered by the President for its protection having positively refused to obey the order.

" 12. In short, the whole state of things borders very closely upon anarchy ; and although in other parts of the Republic lawlessness and inhumanity are less rampantly exhibited, the machinery of administration is everywhere all but paralysed, and the Republic seems about to fall to pieces through its own weakness.

" 13. In that event, the Boers in each district would either have to make their own terms with the adjacent Kaffir tribes, or trek onwards into the wilderness, as is their wont, whilst the position of the large number of British subjects scattered about on farms, or resident in the towns and at the Gold Fields, might fairly claim the humane consideration of Her Majesty's Government even if there were not other reasons for interposing to save so fine a country from so miserable a fate."

In the information supplied to Parliament and to be

found in the different Blue Books, it is conclusively proved that the war then carried on by the Boers was conducted in the most cruel and barbarous manner. As an illustration I quote from the Blue Book C 1776, p. 15.

"There is no doubt that what Turkey is to the rest of Europe, the Transvaal is to the remainder of South Africa. Both countries are centuries behind the civilisation of the day; both are out of sympathy with, yea we may use a stronger word and say, that both are determinedly opposed to, the sentiments and policy of all educated and Christian nations." Both, "by virtue of their religion and by virtue of that idea of superiority which it encourages, have remained as they were long ago, except where partial changes have been forced upon them from without." Since the Boers are Christians it will be incomprehensible to many how this comparison can hold, and yet it is so. Nothing is clearer than that the Boers regard themselves as the elect of heaven, and their particular formularies and mode of worship as rendering them, *par excellence*, the people of God. No Mussulman treats with greater superciliousness the religion of the Christian than does the Transvaal Boer the style of worship followed by his fellow Christians of another school of thought. In his ignorance of history and geography, the farmer of to-day looks upon himself as the lineal descendant of the Jewish patriarch, to whom was given the vocation of a peculiar separation from the world, together with the legacy of superior spiritual privileges. The "stand by, for I am holier than thou" is apparent in all the relations of the Boers with men of other nations and churches.

"The whole world may know it, for it is true, and investigation will only bring out the horrible details, that through the whole course of this Republic's existence it has acted in contravention of the Sand River Treaty ; and slavery has occurred, not only here and there in isolated cases, but as an unbroken practice has been one of the peculiar institutions of the country, mixed up with all its social and political life. It has been at the root of most of its wars ; it has been carried on regularly even in the times of peace.

"It has been characterised by all those circumstances which have so often roused the British nation to an indignant protest and to repeated efforts to banish the slave-trade from the world. The Boers have not only fallen upon unsuspecting kraals simply for the purpose of obtaining the women and children and cattle, but they have carried on a traffic through natives, who have kidnapped the children of their weaker neighbours and sold them to the white man. Again, the Boers have sold and exchanged their victims amongst themselves. Waggon=loads of slaves have been conveyed from one end of the country to the other for sale, and that with the cognisance of, and for the direct advantage of, the higher officials of the land. The writer has himself seen in a town situated in the south of the Republic the children who had been brought down from a remote northern district."

But more authoritative than all, and most interesting at this time, is it to know what was the conviction of

Her Majesty's Government with regard to these matters, and we learn from the concise despatch of the Earl of Carnarvon to Governor Sir Henry Barkly, dated January 25, 1877, that the Boer Government had manifested towards that of Her Majesty just the same reckless disregard of all warnings, friendly advice or remonstrance, that President Kruger and his Hollanders of to-day exhibit in response to the good offices of our Colonial Department. This despatch is of such importance, and so illustrative of the circumstances which induced Lord Carnarvon's action, that I have appended it in full : *

"No. 20.

"The EARL OF CARNARVON to Governor Sir H. BARKLY, G.C M.G., K.C.B.

"DOWNING STREET, *January* 25, 1877.

"SIR,

"I have received your despatches of the 11th December and of the 18th of that month,† on the subject of the barbarous mode in which the hostilities undertaken by the President of the South African Republic against the natives have been conducted.

"2. Her Majesty's Government, after having given full consideration to all the information attainable on the subject, and with every desire to view matters in the most favourable light, deeply regret that they are forced to come to the conclusion that the barbarities alleged to have been committed, though denied by the Transvaal Government, have in fact occurred.

"3. Warnings against this wholly gratuitous and

* See Blue Book C 1776, p. 25.   † Nos. 13 and 16.

unjust war, earnest and friendly advice and finally remonstrances, have been offered by Her Majesty's Government; they have all been ineffectual to arrest the course to which the Transvaal Government seems to have committed itself, leading, as it must, to national bankruptcy and anarchy, but most dangerous to all the neighbouring European communities, whose interests have already been gravely affected by these reckless proceedings.

" 4. Such being the case, it is to be feared that nothing that can be further urged in the way of protest will be of much avail. Nevertheless, it is the duty of Her Majesty's Government again to protest in the plainest and strongest terms possible against the proceedings of the Transvaal Government and the prosecution of this so-called war on the lines of action hitherto adopted; and while I approve of the remonstrance which you have already addressed to President Burgers, I have to instruct you once more to express to him the deep regret and indignation with which Her Majesty's Government view the proceedings of the armed force which is acting in the name and under the authority of the Transvaal Government, and to cause him to understand that he is rapidly making impossible the continuance either of those sentiments of respect and confidence towards him, or of those friendly relations with him as the chief of a neighbouring Government which it was the earnest hope of Her Majesty's Government to preserve.

" 5. I am aware that very many of the inhabitants of the Transvaal deplore as deeply as I do these unhappy occurrences, nor do I suppose that any, except those who are urged by strong personal or political motives, would do otherwise than condemn and put aside the system of which they have been the result. Some, indeed, of the inhabitants (as, for example, in the Lydenburg district) appeal directly to my sympathies and anxieties as British subjects; but, in dealing officially with the responsibilities of the Republic in this matter, I cannot separate the private individuals from the Government which represents them, with whom alone I can remonstrate, and in whose hands is the power of granting redress.

"6. Under the peculiar and critical circumstances which now exist, I propose to await the result of Sir T. Shepstone's mission to Pretoria before instructing you to take any further steps beyond conveying to President Burgers the further protest which I am compelled by a sense of public duty to make through you, and in the plainest and most unequivocal terms.

"I have, &c.,

"(Signed)   "CARNARVON.

"Sir HENRY BARKLY."

Now it has been frequently alleged by Boer propagandists and by those others who have attempted to palliate Mr. Gladstone's line of conduct in 1881, as well as his subsequent surrender in 1884 of all the most important articles of the Convention of 1881, which he and his Cabinet had formally imposed, that Sir T. Shepstone was delegated to Pretoria expressly to carry out a "hobby" of the late Earl of Carnarvon, originally suggested and matured in detail by Sir Bartle Frere—this hobby being nothing less than that the

B

South African Republic was to be driven, if necessary by force of arms, into joining in a grand scheme of confederation of all the South African States ; and, failing this, that the country was to be annexed to the British Crown, that Sir Bartle Frere was sent as High Commissioner to Cape Town to effect this annexation, and that Sir T. Shepstone acted in Pretoria under his instructions !

There is not a shadow of truth in any of the above allegations.

As a matter of fact, Sir Bartle Frere did not reach Cape Town from England until March 31, 1877, and Sir T. Shepstone had actually been in Pretoria from January 22 of the same year, whilst his proclamation annexing the Republic was issued on April 12. So that before Sir Bartle Frere set foot on African soil, the whole of the arrangements for supplanting the Boer Government of the country had been already made by Sir T. Shepstone.

We have only to read the despatches sent to the Home Government long before Sir Bartle Frere came on the scene, by such men as Sir H. Barkly and Sir Henry Bulwer, and Lord Carnarvon's replies thereto, to learn how Her Majesty's advisers were compelled, against their own desires, to take the line they did.

Those measures, which they were driven to adopt, had been forced on them by a situation created by the Boers themselves, and their policy was formed mainly on the long array of stern facts as reported by high responsible British officials in South Africa.

A study of these documents as contained in Blue Books presented to our Houses of Parliament cannot fail to convince any unbiased person of the patient consideration, repeated warnings, and friendly advice given by Lord Carnarvon to the Boer Government. It was only when at length he became thoroughly roused to the imminent danger threatening our people and Colonies by further delay that he assented to Sir T. Shepstone's mission.

Hence, on October 5, 1876, a commission was issued—"under the Royal Sign Manual and Signet appointing Sir Theophilus Shepstone, K.C.M.G., to be a Special Commissioner to inquire respecting disturbances which have taken place in the territories adjoining the Colony of Natal, and empowering him in certain events to exercise the power and jurisdiction of Her Majesty over such territories, or some of them.* No man ever had a freer hand granted by a Government than had this gentleman, and deservedly so, for during his forty years' experience of South Africa as an official he had earned the respect and confidence of both Boers and native chiefs alike. And no man was more competent to bring about a *modus vivendi* between the Crown and the Transvaal State, to the peace of each Colony and Republic in South Africa.

Between Sir T. Shepstone's departure from England and his arrival in Natal, the position had become still more alarming, and he decided accordingly to proceed to Pretoria without delay.

From the moment he entered Transvaal territory until he arrived at the capital of the State, he was received with acclamation *en route*, and this can readily be understood when we learn what was the actual

* See Blue Book C 1776, p. 1.

condition of the Transvaal at that period, which we can best do from Sir T. Shepstone's own words. In a letter to Lord Carnarvon dated Pretoria, March 6, 1877, he says : *

"It was patent, however, to every observer to observe that the Government was powerless to control either its white citizens or its native subjects, and that it was incapable of enforcing its laws or of collecting its taxes ; that the Treasury was empty ; that the salaries of officials had been and are for months in arrears ; and that sums payable for the ordinary and necessary expenditure of Government cannot be had ; and that payment for such services as postal contracts were long and hopelessly overdue ; that the white inhabitants had become split into factions ; that the large native population within the boundaries of the State ignore its authority and laws, and that the powerful ruling king, Cetewayo, is anxious to seize upon the first opportunity of attacking a country, the conduct of whose warriors at Sekukuni's mountains has convinced him that it can be easily conquered by his clamouring regiments.

"During my stay at Pretoria I have had numerous interviews with all classes of the inhabitants of the Republic. None have denied the unfortunate condition of the country, or the state of collapse into which the Government has fallen in consequence of that condition. In all these interviews the most friendly feeling has been exhibited ; the great majority of the people with whom I have spoken see no remedy that can be

* See Blue Book C 1776, p 107.

extracted from the country itself. A few such as Paul Kruger, the only opposing candidate to Mr. Burgers for the position of President, expressed a 'strong hope' or a 'confident belief' that all will come right in time, but no one has any plan and the state of affairs is daily becoming worse."

And further in a letter to the Earl of Carnarvon, dated March 12, 1877,* Sir T. Shepstone states :—

"5. Financially the country is in a state of bankruptcy; commerce can scarcely be said to exist, the taxes are in serious arrear, some will not, some cannot, pay them, and the Government offers to take promissory notes for such small sums even as £10, on bonds upon the debtor's land. The public treasury is absolutely empty, the most pressing demands cannot be met, except by promises and compoundings which but increase the debt. Two instances which have been brought to my notice will illustrate this :—(1) A sum of £2500 was due to one of the post contractors, exclusive of one of £760 previously due, and yet remaining unpaid; the Government being pressed promised by bond to pay £1500 in a fortnight and the balance of £1000 in a month, or forfeit £200; the fortnight has passed, but £600 only was forthcoming. (2) The Volksraad, which had been in session, broke up last week, and the members were much inconvenienced, because there was no money in the treasury to pay their travelling expenses.

"6. These instances, and the action of the Govern-

* See Blue Book C 1776, p. 125

ment show that there is no probability that the larger engagements of the country are likely to be met. Claims of all kinds are daily being presented which cannot be liquidated, either wholly or in part, and the interest on the Railway and Commercial Bank loans is already in arrear.

"7. To estimate correctly the inherent weakness of the State with reference to the native races, it is but necessary to consider the position, strength, and circumstances of the white population, as compared with the position, strength, and temper of the black.

"8. The white strength consists, at the outside, of 8000 men capable of bearing arms, of these about 1000 live in towns and villages, and 350 are the foreign and fluctuating population collected at the goldfields; the remaining 6650 are all farmers, widely scattered in isolated homesteads over a surface equal to that of Great Britain and Ireland put together.

"9. These 6650 farmers are the only producers which the Republic has to depend upon for resources and supplies of every kind, and they constitute also the military strength of the State. The goldfields are undeveloped, and furnish too uncertain data to be as yet of much account in any estimate of the permanent producing or military power of the country.

"10. When any native demonstration has to be met or rebellion suppressed, the farmers have to leave their farms and do the work of soldiers; the few bees that make the little honey that is made in this country have to cease their productive labours, and the immediate effect is that the income of the State is cut off at a moment when its expenditure must be indefinitely, and may be enormously, increased. The Sikukuni war has been a notable example of this. Insignificant in its dimensions when compared with what might happen, and with what must happen before long, if a change is not made in the strength of the State, this little episode in its history has proved serious enough to bring about utter bankruptcy and collapse, and had not the farmers mutinied against their President and other leaders at Sikukuni's mountain as they did, and when they did, it is not improbable that the calamity of famine would have been added to the disastrous consequences."

To dispose effectually of the charge brought against Her Majesty's Government that the Boers had to be coerced into confederation or annexation to carry out Lord Carnarvon's "hobby," I here append the special Commissioner's account as to the army accompanying him to Pretoria and also as to the forces at his disposal.*

" 12. The protest, the minute and decision of the Executive Council, as well as the proclamation by Mr. Burgers, were necessary to calm strong feeling here and there, but the great value of them has been that of furnishing an excuse to the great body of the people to accept quietly what they feel is the only means of saving themselves and the country.

" 13. In the resolution or minute of the Executive Council my act is described as one of 'violence.' It seems to me to be necessary only to state that the Transvaal is about the same size as Great Britain and

* See Blue Book C 1776, p. 154, pars. 12 and 13, Appendix.

Ireland put together; that it is believed to contain a population of 40,000 whites and 800,000 natives; that I entered this territory with my personal staff only and an escort of 25 Natal mounted policemen on the 4th January, and after a slow progress reached Pretoria, the capital, on the 22nd January last; that I have never hesitated during these three months and more to explain to both the Government and the people the condition of the State, and the only remedy that appeared to me capable of saving it from immediate ruin; that I have again and again expressed my willingness to at once withdraw if any plan or action or latent power in the country could be shown me by which its independence could be saved and maintained, and the dangers to its neighbours be averted, but without result; that I have invariably been and still am treated with the utmost deference and respect by all classes of the people; and that the only means by which I could have used violence in carrying out what I have done—*i.e.*, Her Majesty's troops—were four weeks march from me in the Colony of Natal, and cannot be here even now within a fortnight, or very nearly a month after the issue of my proclamation, and of my having assumed the Government. These facts will, I think, show your Lordship conclusively that I have acted in accordance with the real convictions and feelings of the people, and that for an officer accompanied, as I was, by a staff of twelve gentlemen and an escort of twenty-five men, openly and avowedly to attempt to subvert the Government of a country and place himself at its head against the true wishes of such a people would have been an act of madness."

In the same despatch he states :

" Every step I have taken towards the accomplishment of my object was taken with the knowledge of the President. I thought it my duty to be perfectly open and frank with him from the beginning, and on the last occasion of my meeting him in the Executive Council he took the opportunity to acknowledge and thank me for what he was good enough to call my considerate and frank behaviour to him and the Government."

The only opposition which appears to have been made to annexation was offered by a small number of the Executive, but even then, with the exception of Mr. Paul Kruger, all came in afterwards.

Sir T. Shepstone says in this same despatch :

" The officers of the late Republic including every member of the Executive Council *except Mr. Paul Kruger*, one of the delegates appointed to go to Europe, have all signified in writing their willingness to serve under the new form of Government."

But Sir T. Shepstone had met with another kind of opposition and from a quarter not previously anticipated. Several Hollanders had been previously introduced into the Republic by President Burgers and we find that these persons did all in their power to stir up strife, as will be seen from the following excerpt from Sir T. Shepstone's despatch : *

" 8. Every effort had been made during the previous

* See Blue Book C 1776, p. 153.

fortnight by, it is said, educated Hollanders residing at the seat of Government, and who had but lately arrived in the country, to rouse the fanaticism of the Boers, and to induce them to offer 'bloody' resistance to what it was known I intended to do. The Boers were appealed to in the most inflammatory language by printed manifestos and memorials; agents were sent out to excite them by violent speeches at public meetings, and every possible means were used to intimidate individuals, and stifle the expression of real opinion; it was urged that I had but a small escort, which could be easily overpowered, and that there would be no difficulty in putting the mission across the border; but, as I had judged from the first, the daily accumulating pressure and personal distress which the circumstances of the country were bringing upon them had created in the minds of the people a conviction that the State did not possess inherent vitality enough to relieve them, and that the only prospect of relief lay in their accepting my proposal. Every intelligent man, from the highest to the lowest, with whom I discussed the question frankly admitted this, and those who opposed my mission because of their positions in the State were equally frank in the expression in that direction of their personal opinions; I know, therefore, that in spite of the efforts to create opposition there was at bottom no feeling strong enough to nourish it; and my judgment has been so far confirmed by the fact that from the moment that the proclamation was published to this, opposition has been gradually dying away, and the disposition to accept the situation growing apace.

" 9. Immediately after the issue of the proclamation Mr. Burgers addressed the assembled officials and, in taking leave of them, urged them to loyally serve the new Government, he directed Mr. Swart, the State Secretary, to hand over formally to me the key of the offices, a direction which he (Mr. Swart) at once came to the house I occupy to comply with, and upon his doing so I handed it back to his charge."

It would be manifestly unfair to the Boers were we not to consider the situation from their side, for, during the negotiations with Sir T. Shepstone, the Volksraad was in session at Pretoria, and President Burgers several times addressed that assembly on these all-important questions, especially on the 3rd and 5th March. No authority in the land could emphasise or explain the position to his countrymen so well as their Chief Magistrate. He performed a painful task with great courage, and his utterances were so clear, and expressed in language so unmistakeable, that I give extracts from his speeches delivered on the occasions mentioned.*

"We should delude ourselves by entertaining the hope that matters would mend by-and-by. It would be only self-deceit. I tell you openly, matters are as bad as they ever can be ; they cannot be worse. These are bitter truths, and people may perhaps turn their back on me. But then I shall have the consolation of having done my duty."

*   *   *   *

" Do you know what has recently happened in

* See Blue Book C 1776, pp. 160, 162, and 163.

Turkey ?   Because no civilised Government was carried
on there the Great Powers interfered and said, Thus
far and no further.   And if this is done to an Empire,
will a little Republic be excused when it misbehaves ?
Complain to other powers and seek justice there ?
Yes, thank God ! justice is still to be found even for the
most insignificant ; but it is precisely this justice which
will convict us.   If we want justice we must be in a
position to ask it with unsullied hands.   (Cheers.)"

     *   *   *   *

"Whence has arisen that urgency to make an appeal
for interference elsewhere ?   Has that appeal been
made only by enemies of the State ?   Oh no, gentlemen, it has arisen from real grievances.   Our people
have degenerated from their former position, they have
become demoralised, they are not what they ought to
be.   (Cheers.)"

     *   *   *   *

"To-day a bill for £1100 was laid before me for
signature, but I would sooner have cut off my right
hand than sign that paper (cheers), for I have not the
slightest ground to expect that when the bill becomes
due there will be a penny to pay it with."

     *   *   *   *

"The principal thing which had brought them to
their present position was that to which they would not
give attention ; it was not this or that thing which
impeded their way, but they themselves stopped the
way, and if they asked him what prevented the people
from remaining independent, he answered that the
Republic was itself the obstruction, owing to the
inherent incapacity and weakness of the people.   But

whence this weakness? Was it because they were deformed? Because they were worse than other people? Because they were too few and insignificant to occupy the country? Those arguments did not weigh with him, they were not true, he did not consider them of any importance. The people were as good as any other people, but they were completely demoralised, they had lost faith in God, reliance upon themselves, or trust in each other, hence he believed they were inherently weak."

    *   *   *   *

"In several of the cities of Holland there were people who had subscribed for only one debenture, because they thought men of their own blood were living in South Africa. What was the consequence? The interest up to July last had been paid; in January of this year £2250 was due for interest, and there was not a penny to meet it.

"To take up arms and 'fight was nonsense; to draw the sword would be to draw the sword against God, for it was God's judgment that the State was in the condition it was to-day (cheers), and it was their duty to inquire whether they should immerse in blood the thousands of innocent inhabitants of this country, and if so, what for? For an idea; something they had in their heads, but not in their hearts; for an independence which is not prized? Let them make the best of the situation, and get the best terms they possibly could; let them agree to join their hands to those of their brethren on the south, and then from the Cape to the Zambesi there would be one great people. Yes, there was something grand in that, grander even than their idea of a Republic, something which ministered to their national feeling (cheers), and would this be so miserable? Yes, this would be miserable for those who would not be under the law, for the rebel and the revolutionist, but welfare and prosperity for the men of law and order."

*   *   *   *

"They must not underrate their real and many difficulties. He could point to the South-western border, the Zulu, the Gold Fields, and other questions, and show them that it was their duty to come to an arrangement with the British Government, and to do so in a bold and manly manner. An hon. member on Saturday last had spoken of fervent patriotism, but he had failed to appreciate the reference because it amounted to this, that they must shut their eyes to everything, so as to keep their independence."

On April 12, 1877, Sir T. Shepstone issued his proclamation formally annexing the country as a colony of the Crown, subject to the conditions set forth therein.*

True it is that a protest was made by the Boer Executive Council on April 11,† but this appears to have been more a formality than anything else, as we learn from Sir T. Shepstone's account thereof.‡

"On Wednesday, the 11th inst., the Attorney-General and Chief Clerk came and officially read the

---

* See Blue Book C 1776.
† See Blue Book C 1776, p. 156, and Appendix.
‡ P. 153, par. 4, Despatch April 17, and Appendix.

protest to me, and at the same time handed in a resolution of the Executive Council, copy of each herewith enclosed, from which it appeared that, in addition to the protest, a mission to Her Majesty's Government, and contingently to other governments which had acknowledged the independence of the State, had been determined upon. The resolution appointed the Attorney-General, E. J. P. Jorissen, LL.D., and Mr. Paul Kruger, Vice-President, to be members of this mission, with power to add a third person if required. I received these papers, but as they contained nothing to induce me to change the view I had taken of my duty, I said that while I recognised the propriety of their discharging what they conceived to be incumbent upon them, I must ask them to do the same with regard to me ; they expressed their acquiescence, and the interview, which had been friendly throughout, ended.

" Mr. Burgers called upon me shortly afterwards and explained to me the object of these documents."

In pursuance of that protest, however, the Hon. S. P. J. Kruger, Vice-President of the Republic, and the Hon. the Attorney-General, Doctor E. J. P. Jorissen, were delegated to proceed to England. These gentlemen were well received in this country, but failed entirely in the object of their mission, nor did another deputation in 1878, also headed by Mr. Kruger, meet with better success.

CHAPTER III

EVENTS PRIOR TO THE CONVENTION

THE annexation of the Transvaal having duly taken place in 1877 under the circumstances that I have described, we must now pass to the events which resulted in our defeat at Majuba Hill and the signing of the Convention of 1881.

Although Mr. Kruger and his Boer companions, aided by their Hollander coadjutors, did not convince either Lord Carnarvon or, later, Sir Michael Hicks Beach (his successor at the Colonial Office) that the Transvaal would be better governed by a few immaculate Boers and Hollanders than under the British Crown, their visits to England proved highly beneficial to the objects they had in view.

A very short residence here enabled them to discover that for party purposes a strong Radical faction was ready and willing to denounce Lord Carnarvon's policy and what was termed his " Federation Scheme," the policy, by the way, which to-day in relation to our Colonies is almost universally applauded and advocated.

Mr. Kruger and his associates had, figuratively speaking, fallen on velvet. They promptly took in the situation, hailed with delight this political ring of "little Englanders" as champions of the innocent Boers, victims of Tory oppression, and with all their might they aided this group to discredit the recent acts of its opponents.

Whilst thus co-operating with the Radical faction, a strong impression was produced on their minds by our usual, lamentable want of union on Imperial and Colonial questions in face of an enemy, and of which they have invariably taken advantage. Mr. Kruger then felt, and has since always acted on the assumption, that if a Conservative Government held office in England, every effort would be made by the opposition to weaken or impede any measures which might be proposed to compel him to observe his pledges or obligations.

Deep in his heart this rugged old Boer has the utmost contempt for our so-called patriotism and for the tactics displayed for purely party ends regardless of the national honour or the rights of Uitlanders in the South African Republic.

On their arrival here a second time, the Boer delegates found that a problem awaited solution which to the Government of the day was of far greater importance than even the future of a large English-speaking population extending from Cape Town to the limitless north. This question occupied the minds of Her Majesty's Ministers to the exclusion of almost all other Imperial or Colonial matters—Ireland was the cry! Agitators abounded, and in and out of Parliament the sorrows and woes of one or more sections of these down-trodden victims of English tyranny were daily

paraded. Arguments still more forcible were being
brought to bear with a frequency which became
monotonous, yet none the less terrible in their effect on
the public mind. Constituted authority and the law
were being daily set at defiance, and a rooted objection
to the payment of rent or taxes was emphasised by the
shooting of landlords and officials from behind a
wall. The cabins of suspected informers were being
raided and their inmates foully murdered, and by the
judicious application of explosives to private dwellings
it was sought to strike terror into the hearts of all.
Small wonder then that these astute gentlemen from
Africa and Holland quickly grasped the situation.
A very slight stretch of imagination was requisite to
institute a parallel in their minds between the wrongs
of Irish malcontents and those which they considered
had invariably been inflicted on their race by England.
Neither was any great discernment needed to discover
the weak points in our armour. They perceived that
the Government which a short time before had stepped
in to protect the Boers against themselves was tottering
to its fall, and they recognised fully that when the
Liberal party came into office a firm Colonial policy
would assuredly form no part of its programme.

The lessons thus learnt were invaluable to Paul
Kruger, who had only one aim in view, one object to
accomplish, at all risks and by any means—the South
African Republic to be governed solely by Boers,
independently of the Crown! Is he to be blamed for
his dogged determination in pursuit of this idea?

On his return to Pretoria with the rich store of
knowledge and experience thus garnered, he could

afford to bide his time and wait an opportunity. No man understood his fellow Boers as well as he. Recognised as the head of the powerful religious sect known as Doppers, he exercised a commanding influence over all those who belonged to that branch of the Dutch Reformed Church, and he was thoroughly convinced that, when he called upon them, they would rally round him to a man.

Meanwhile, the natives within and on the Transvaal borders had become more menacing. Sir T. Shepstone had been withdrawn from Pretoria and his post filled by a military official, Colonel Sir William Lanyon. As we have seen, for some time prior to the annexation, Cetewayo, King of the Zulus, had given clear proofs of uneasiness and of his desire for war. At length his conduct became so outrageous that we were compelled to take hostile measures against him for the protection both of Natal and the Transvaal. After many sanguinary encounters our operations ultimately ended, in 1879, in the subjugation of the Zulu nation and in the capture of its ruler.

Moreover, in that year Sir Garnet Wolseley had been appointed High Commissioner in South Africa, and he had found it necessary to reduce to subjection a chief named Umbeline, who had been giving great trouble, as well as Sikukuni, who ever since the Boers had failed to defeat him in 1876 and 1877, had remained within his strongholds and become a standing menace to the peace of South Africa.

Whilst these operations were in progress, a strict watch had to be kept on the large Kaffir tribes in the northern and eastern portions of the Transvaal, and

British garrisons were established in different districts at long distances from each other.

Mr. Kruger and a few Boer leaders clearly saw how difficult it would be to concentrate these scattered forces at any given point, and also how easily they could be attacked and dealt with in detail, or when on the march. They secretly and determinedly set to work, therefore, to organise commandos of disaffected Boers throughout the Veldt. Ammunition was purchased and hoarded in every waggon, and the word was passed where each party was to assemble.

All that now remained was to find a fitting excuse for the revolt, and to fix upon the day on which to throw off the mask.

A reason which could be alleged for taking up arms had long been present to the clear shrewd minds of Paul Kruger and his friends, and had indeed been communicated to every Boer as an inducement to join the ranks of the disaffected. It can be explained in one word—taxes.

Now, payment of taxes may be said to be regarded by the majority, even in the most civilised communities, as a hardship to be borne, but to a Boer it is a monstrous injustice. In the days before annexation took place he had always resented every demand made on him by the tax-gatherer as a personal wrong. One can appreciate the difficulties besetting a revenue collector in his attempts to convince a gentleman on the Veldt with a waggon for his home, that the latter should contribute towards maintaining the Government at Potchefstroom, and how still more onerous would be his task, under the circumstances, to recover such tax by any known process of law.   True, when he went into a town or to a nachtmal, a sort of religious assembly, an attempt would sometimes be made to compel this recalcitrant personage to pay his dues, but he invariably shirked the demand on one plea or another.   The Boers never had any properly organised collection of their revenue, everything was left more or less to chance, and the salaries of officials were so miserably small that it was absolutely worth no one's while in outlying districts thus to serve the State.

This condition of affairs had to be remedied when the Transvaal came under British administration.   Soon the Boers learnt that they were expected to pay taxes for the protection afforded them, yet they never could or would comprehend that, if a Government was to exist, money must be found.   Even their bitter experience of the abject state of national degradation and bankruptcy to which they had sunk, and which had led to annexation by the Crown, taught them no lesson. Previously, taxes had been almost invariably collected from foreigners, commercial men, and residents in towns only, therefore, those Boers living on farms scattered over the Veldt could not appreciate the need for any change in the system, so that when, under the new *régime*, they were called on to contribute their quota towards the expenses of administration, they fiercely resented to a man what they regarded as an extortion. Paul Kruger and his friends experienced no difficulty in fanning this flame, and an important part was played in the movement by those wily Hollanders, also, who in 1878 had given so much trouble to Sir T. Shepstone.

Unjust taxation, then, was the flimsy pretext advanced to cover the real object Paul Kruger determined to achieve—self-government by Boers independently of the Crown.

Lord Beaconsfield's Cabinet had fallen early in 1880, and Mr. Gladstone had succeeded him as Prime Minister; the time was therefore ripe. Mr. Kruger was well aware that no strenuous effort would be made by Great Britain to retain the remote colony as an appanage of the Empire ; only a bold dash was required whilst the British troops available in South Africa were few, and the Boers could then demand their own terms.

The plan previously concerted was to cut off all British garrisons, confine them to their various stations and hold the roads, so as to prevent any reinforcements from reaching them. But until some special act of injustice could be alleged as a reason for armed resistance, it is obvious that the Boers had no excuse to move. However, when so desired, a pretext was not far to seek. One Bezuidenhout had been served with a notice to pay £27 5s. by the Landdrost of Potchefstroom, which he refused to do, at the same time tendering £14. Judgment was given against him and his waggon was attached for the amount due. This circumstance was seized upon as a sample of the outrages perpetrated on these honest and simple farmers.

Again I leave the story to be told by those who were on the spot at the time, and whose knowledge was better than any to which we can aspire.* Sir Owen

* See Blue Book 2783, p 19 ; Report of Mr. Hudson, Colonial Secretary, p. 24, and Appendix.

Lanyon in a despatch to Lord Kimberley, dated December 5, 1880, makes the following statement:

"In continuation of my despatch of the 28th November, I have the honour to forward further reports received from Mr. Hudson relative to the action of certain Boers at Potchefstroom who resisted the law.

"A perusal of these reports will show your Lordship that the Government has spared no means in order that a peaceful termination may be arrived at in this matter. I consider that Mr. Hudson's action was one which was well worthy of your Lordship's approbation, for he incurred considerable personal risk in going out as he did to meet Mr. Kruger.

"The report of the interview serves to prove what I have already pointed out, that neither the leaders nor the people know what they want further than that they object to pay taxes, or to be subordinate to the laws of the State. A re-perusal of the former reports of interviews between officials and these people will show that the arguments now used by Mr. Kruger are the same as those advanced on every similar occasion since the annexation, now two years and eight months ago. They seem to forget or to ignore the fact that the State must be supported, and that it cannot allow a portion of its citizens to set at naught such obligations till such times as it may be convenient to them to act up to them. All of them make ready use of its institutions when they want to do so; and when it suits their convenience or ends one does not hear of their protest preventing their taking advantage of that improved state of government and of affairs which Her Majesty's rule has conferred upon them. I do not know of a single instance in which any of them threw up an office of emolument because of their principles, and I can mention many who whilst opposing the Government held on to the office of Field Cornet, and continued to draw their £50 per annum as long as they could. Notwithstanding, some of these men tried to avoid paying their taxes on the grounds that they were protesting against the Government. In no instance, however, did their conscientious scruples prompt them to object to receive money from Her Majesty's Government. *Mr. Kruger's case exemplifies this, for he continued to draw salary as a member of the Executive Council for a period of 8½ months after the annexation. In fact, he would doubtless have been drawing it now, for, notwithstanding his term of office expired on the 4th November, 1877, he applied for and received pay up to the close of the year.* Mr. C. J. Joubert, another of the leaders, acted in precisely the same manner. Not long since Mr. Hemming Pretorius, who had been Field Cornet for some time after the annexation, applied for arrears of his pay to the Treasurer, though he knew that he had refused to pay his taxes.

" The Committee has now settled that the mass meeting shall take place a month earlier than was intended. It is to be held on the 8th, at a farm called Paardeplaats, which is about 35 miles from here in the Potchefstroom direction.

" Every endeavour is being made in order to get as many as possible to attend it, and (as was the practice regarding former meetings) threats and intimidation are freely used to force the people to attend. I have received frequent reports to this effect. Several loyal Boers have been to see me to ask for protection, because emissaries had been to them threatening that their houses would be burnt down if they did not attend. In fact, a reign of terror exists, and this renders it impossible for the Government to obtain evidence sufficient to prosecute these men.

"But this action on the part of the agitation in forcing unwilling men to attend the meeting is an element of safety, for it will strengthen the ranks of those who are opposed to overt acts of rebellion. I do not think that the leaders wish for warlike measures, for they have too much to lose. Nevertheless, they are responsible for having kept up the agitation, and for bringing together the elements of discord. They have brought their followers to the brink of a precipice, and I trust they may have sufficient power to make them look before they leap.

"I still do not think there is much cause for anxiety, but the position of affairs is one which requires careful attention and watching.

"I append a copy of the instructions I caused to be issued to Major Clarke upon his assuming the charge of the Potchefstroom district.

I have, &c.

"(Signed)   "W. OWEN LANYON,

"*Administrator.*

"The Right Hon. the EARL OF KIMBERLEY."

That this allegation of unjust enforcement of taxes was of the most flimsy character, and only used as an excuse to veil their real motives, is plainly apparent from the conduct of these disaffected Boers towards their own Government, before Her Majesty was compelled to step in, literally, to save them from themselves. That burghers in outlying districts refused to pay taxes was only natural, and particularly when they knew that members of the Volksraad were the greatest delinquents in this direction. That this utter disregard of the law, and of their obligations towards the maintenance of constituted authority, had been going on for years is evident from the resolutions of the Volksraad itself, and from the plain statements made to their faces by President Burgers. Let us take a few illustrations.*

" *Volksraad Session*, 1868.   *February* 12, 1868, *Art.* 255.

" Put to the order Art. III. of the financial report, viz. :

" The Committee find by the general statement of the public income for the financial year 1866, drawn by the Auditor-General, that the collections of the poll-tax and quit-rent on farms and Erven of the different districts, particularly Potchefstroom, Pretoria and Lydenburg, are comparatively very small, and that for this reason the State President may be directed that the arrears and annual taxes are properly collected according to law.

" The Volksraad resolve to adopt Art. III. of the financial report, with amendment of the last portion as follows :

" That his honour the State President is charged to direct the landdrosts to collect all taxes without delay, and that if not complying with the orders of those

* See Blue Book 2783, pp. 46 and 47.

placed above them they shall be liable to a fine of from £15 to £50 for the first time, and on a repetition they shall be discharged."

"Volksraad Session, 1871. December 2, 1871, Art. 426 C.

"The Committee for the estimates recommended that from now henceforth all persons who are negligent in paying their taxes at the time stipulated shall, after an elapse of six months after the taxes are due, pay double the amount."

The following resolution was passed by the Volksraad in March 1877:

"Whereas it appears from the report of the Financial Commission that the greater part of the taxes have not been paid, and as it is therefore impossible to carry on the Government of the country, the Volksraad resolves to authorise the Government to collect all outstanding taxes, not by the ordinary procedure adopted in civil cases, but by summary process."

Extract from President's Speech at opening of Volksraad, February 13, 1877.

"As a matter of course, the state of our finances first demands attention. With deep regret I have openly to state that our expectation when passing the annual estimates, as also the special estimates for the war expenses, have not been realised by far, for reasons which I will explain further on. This will be clear to you from a perusal of the documents, which will in connection therewith be brought to your notice."

Extract from Speech of President Burgers, in Volksraad, on February 16, 1877.

"Two causes, viz., our position towards the natives (the Secocoeni war), the financial embarrassment of the Government, and its subsequent helplessness. What is now to be done? Methinks no more nor less than remove these grievances. Get the native under due authority, restrict him in his savage ways, and strengthen your Government by obedience to the laws and by fulfilling your duty as burghers, and then, I assure you, you shall hear no more of confederation."

*   *   *   *

"As long as I am bound by my oath and the people are indeed with me, I shall do what I can for our liberty. But if they want independence without fulfilling their duty as burghers, and obedience to law and order, then we must bid good-bye to our liberty."

Extract from Speech of President, February 20, 1877.

"Public meetings had been held in presence of members of the Volksraad, where it had been unanimously resolved not to pay the taxes. How could the officials carry out the law in the face of such proceedings? Had he (his honour) to add civil war to all our present miseries? Owing to the request of old and experienced burghers he had ordered the landdrosts only to urge the people to pay their taxes, but not as yet to summon them. And beyond this, how had summonses to be served when here one landdrost was carried out of his office, and there the office door was locked in the face of another, and elsewhere officials were deterred from doing their duty by intimidating crowds at their office."

*   *   *   *

"He thought it most astonishing that hon. members of this Raad should have committed acts which tended to create the greatest rebellion in the country. Here they passed laws and resolutions, not for themselves, but for the burghers outside. Here they imposed taxes which the outsiders had to pay, but which they themselves refused to pay. Must that not lead to the worst anarchy? Could the burghers be expected to obey the laws when they saw those who passed these laws violate the same in such an outrageous manner? The evil must be rooted out. The legislator who breaks one law is guilty of all. The Raad is bound to sift this matter thoroughly."

There can be no doubt of this broad fact that had Bezuidenhout's waggon been returned and the claim on him remitted, the result would have been exactly the same.

A large meeting of Boers had been summoned for January 8, but this was antedated to December 15. At a place called Paardekraal, on the anniversary of their victory over the Kaffir King Dingaan in 1836, armed Boers, acting on secret instructions, assembled in thousands and, then and there, resolved to abolish their Committee appointed previously and to elect departmental officers.

On the 16th of the same month a force of from 4000 to 6000 men took possession of Heidelberg, and proclaimed a Government of their own under the Presidency of Paul Kruger.*

"LANDDROST, Standerton, to his Excellency the GOVERNOR, Pietermaritzburg, Colony Natal.

"*December* 19, 1880.

"Your Excellency will probably not be aware of the Boer movements, as telegraph communication between this and Pretoria has been stopped. I have to inform your Excellency that a Boer force of from 4000 to 6000 men took possession of the town of Heidelberg on the 16th, and established their own Government under the Presidency of Paul Kruger. Piet Joubert is Commandant-General ; Jorissen, Attorney-General ; Bok, Acting State Secretary : Jacob Mare, Landdrost at Heidelberg. Landdrost Neckcrucan was from town when his office was taken possession of, no violence was used; protection offered to the Bank by Boers. The inhabitants of Heidelberg are not allowed to leave, unless supplied with a passport, signed by the State Secretary on behalf of the Commandant-General.

"I will send an express to Pretoria in two hours' time, so can forward any communication your Excellency may wish to send to the Administrator."

How cleverly this rising was arranged, and how opportune the moment chosen for attack, may be gathered from the despatch of Sir G. P. Colley to the Secretary of State for War, dated December 26, 1880.

* See Blue Book C 2783, p. 60.

"1. I regret to have to report that on the 20th instant a portion of the 94th Regiment, consisting of the head-quarters and about 250 men, marching from Lydenburg to Pretoria, were attacked about 37 miles from Pretoria by a large number of Boers, and overpowered; about 120 men are reported killed or wounded, and the rest taken prisoners. The only details yet received are given in the two telegrams of which copies are annexed.

"2. The circumstances of the march of this detachment, so far as known to me, are as follows :

"On the 23rd ultimo, owing to the detachment of troops which it had been found necessary to send from Pretoria to Potchefstroom, and the consequent weakening of the garrison of the former place, a movement of concentration on Pretoria was ordered by the officer commanding the troops in the Transvaal, acting in concert with his Excellency the Administrator. This movement included the withdrawal of one company 94th Regiment, from Marabastadt, and of the head-quarters and two companies of that regiment from Lydenburg; leaving a detachment only at the latter place in charge of the fort and store.

"3. At that time telegraphic communication between Pretoria and my head-quarters was temporarily interrupted; and the movement was therefore carried out without reference to me. It was, however, entirely in accordance with my general views, which were to reduce our detachments and strengthen the moveable force at Pretoria, and I approved of it as soon as it was reported to me.

"4. At the time these movements were ordered, no

apprehension of so sudden, widespread and determined a rising seems to have been felt; orders had been issued against small escorts and parties moving about the country, as it was feared they would be exposed to insult, and accidental collision might ensue; but no serious attack was apprehended. The disturbances at Potchefstroom were of the same character as had taken place on many former occasions; and had their direct origin in the usual cause—the demand for payment of taxes. Gatherings of Boers had been reported, but all of them too small to endanger any considerable detachment of troops; *and the mass meeting long announced, remained fixed for the 8th Jannary, a date still six weeks distant.*

"5. The company from Marabastadt reached its destination punctually and without molestation, but the Lydenburg detachment, which was originally expected at Pretoria about the 12th instant, was delayed by bad roads and flooded rivers, and appears to have been still near Middleburg when the Boer rising took place and Heidelberg was seized. On the 16th the Boer leaders sent in their demands to the Administrator, allowing 48 hours for a reply. In the meanwhile the Boers sent to warn the Officer Commanding at Standerton, that any further advance of troops would be considered a declaration of war. I have not heard whether any similar warning was sent to the Lydenburg detachment, but warning was in any case sent to it by Colonel Bellairs, commanding the troops in the Transvaal. On the 19th the reply of his Excellency the Administrator appears to have been received at Heidelberg, and on the 20th the detachment was attacked.

"6. I have directed the Officer Commanding at Standerton to communicate with the Boers, and ask to be allowed to send a surgeon to attend to the wounded ; and also to endeavour, if possible, to have the wounded sent in to us.   I have little doubt that similar efforts will be made from Pretoria ; and I trust that the Boers will act humanely and give the wounded all care and assistance."

The fact is our officials were either ignorant of the importance of the movement, or were entirely put off their guard by the Boer ruse of giving out that their mass meeting would be held on January 8, whereas they were all fully prepared to strike on December 16. As they had prognosticated, orders had been given to outlying British detachments to march on, and con- centrate at, Pretoria.   Suddenly, the Boers seized Heidelberg and Potchefstroom, and on December 20, fell on a portion of the 94th Regiment and annihi- lated it.

"*From the* OFFICER COMMANDING, *Standerton, to the* GENERAL OFFICER COMMANDING, *Natal and Transvaal.*

"Arrived 8 A.M., travelling through night to escape rebel patrol reported on road, half-way met men from Middelburgh, who said 94th, between that and Pretoria, were met by rebel force 800 or 1000 strong.   A man with white flag demanded their arms. The Commanding Officer refusing, the rebels poured in a volley, and killed seven officers, two wounded, one woman, and 201 men, the rest (49) taken prisoners. The place was a spruit where all waggons had stuck. Ten soldiers and two waggons left to bury dead. I fear this is true, as informants are Barrett Brothers, who had left Middelburgh on seeing the massacre, but could not reach me, being stopped by rebel patrol. ,

"True copy.
"A H. WAVELL, Lieutenant-Colonel, A.A.G.
"Head-Quarters, Pietermaritzburg.
"*January* 26, 1880."

General Sir George Colley moved up from Natal with all his available forces, and on January 26, and again on February 9, he sustained severe checks at the hands of a strong force of Boers. These reverses to the British arms created an exaggerated expression of timidity in the minds of Her Majesty's Ministers at home, and when Sir George Colley telegraphed that he had been approached by the President with a view to a peace, the home authorities became eagerly anxious to fall in with Kruger's offer.* The first sign of this disposition is shown by the following telegram from Lord Kimberley to Sir Hercules Robinson:

"February 16. I have received following telegram from Sir G. Colley: '13th. Letter received from Kruger, purport,—Anxious to make one more effort to stop bloodshed; Boers driven to arms in self-defence; views continually misrepresented; if deed of annexation cancelled, willing co-operate with British Government everything for good of South Africa; know that English people would be on their side if truth reached them;

* See C 2837, p. 10. Secretary of State for Colonies to Governor Sir Hercules Robinson.

are so strong in this conviction that would not fear inquiry of a Royal Commission, which they know would give them their rights; ready, therefore, if troops ordered to withdraw from Transvaal, to give free passage and withdraw from their positions; if annexation upheld will fight to the end.' Telegram ends.

" I replied to-day as follows :—Your telegram 13th received. Inform Kruger that, if Boers will desist from armed opposition, we shall be quite ready to appoint Commissioners with extensive powers, and who may develop the scheme referred to in my telegram to you of the 8th instant. Add that if this proposal is accepted, you are authorised to agree to suspension of hostilities on our part. Message ends.

" Communicate foregoing to President Brand.

" Blyth, Consul Free State, called to-day with important telegram, conveying very friendly assurances from President. I requested him to convey by telegram to President the satisfaction with which I had received this communication."

At this period President Brand of the Orange Free State was in almost daily communication with Her Majesty's Government, and he proffered his services to bring about a settlement with the Boer leaders. This offer was accepted, and he honourably and loyally did his best to fulfil his self-imposed difficult and delicate task.

On February 26, a day that will be long memorable in the annals of the Transvaal, Sir George Colley occupied Majuba Mountain, and on the morning of the 27th he was attacked by a strong force of Boers, who retook the hill and almost destroyed the British troops. In this action the British commander was himself among the slain.

On learning this intelligence, Her Majesty's Ministers seem to have been still more scared than they were before, although Sir Evelyn Wood, who had taken command, telegraphed on March 1 to the Secretary of State for War as follows:

"The promised reinforcements will be ample, even if the Boers are still more largely reinforced; they have not yet taken advantage of temporary advantage, and every hour's respite is a gain."

However, on the same day we find that Lord Kimberley telegraphed to Sir Evelyn Wood:

"Inform me if you know when Sir George Colley made communication to Kruger in pursuance of my telegram of February 16, what time fixed in which answer must be given and whether any, and if so what, communications have since passed between him and Boer leaders."

Again, on March 3, the Government being still nervously anxious, he telegraphed:

"March 3.—My telegram March 1st. If you find that Sir George Colley made communication to Kruger, but no answer has been received, inquire of Boer leaders whether an answer will be sent you."

Then on March 4, Lord Kimberley telegraphed again :

" 4th March.   Your telegram of March 2nd.   State date on which Colley's communication sent to Boers, to whom addressed, and to what place.   Was person to whom sent known to be competent to reply without reference to others ?   Reply as quickly as possible.   I understand from your telegram that no answer has been received from Kruger, and therefore inquiry directed in my telegram of yesterday should still be made."

Sir Evelyn Wood, however, had no such fears as those permeating the minds of Mr. Gladstone and his Cabinet, but felt that under the conditions of our various defeats, this haste to truckle to the Boer leaders was, to his soldierly instincts, most untimely, and we learn he was perfectly convinced that the only way to make peace on a sound and satisfactory basis was after a success in the field by British arms.   He knew that, notwithstanding the defeats at Laings Nek and Majuba, the Boers were only too anxious to bring matters to a conclusion without further fighting, and as speedily as possible.   That this was so we learn from his telegram dated March 5, in reply to that sent by Lord Kimberley on the 4th, as follows :

" Newcastle, March 5th, noon.   I anticipate hearing from Joubert soon.   Fear until Boers are defeated leaders, if altogether excluded from amnesty, will continue hostilities if they can ; but, on the other hand, the very unfavourable weather, and their admitted certainty of eventual suppression may cause dispersion. Sir G. Colley was very averse to pardon leaders, and your telegram of 10th implies such cannot be granted. Instruct me fully on this point, for much will turn on it ; and, reflecting on similar struggles in history, I do not attach much importance to punishing leaders, as did Sir George Colley, though I would not recommend allowing them to remain in Transvaal, nor would I accept them as representatives of people. *In discussing settlement of country, my constant endeavour shall be to carry out the spirit of your orders; but, considering the disasters we have sustained, I think the happiest result will be that, after accelerating successful action, which I hope to fight in about fourteen days, the Boers should disperse without any guarantee, and then many now undoubtedly coerced, will readily settle down.* In any negotiations, Joubert will probably make dispersion contingent on amnesty. I may be cut off from communicating with you, and if you wish to avoid further fighting, I suggest, while giving me no instructions for the future settlement, you should empower me, if absolutely necessary, to promise life and property, but not residence, to leaders. This I would not do, if dispersion could be effected without it."

Even before Sir George Colley's sad death, Mr. Gladstone had stated in the House of Commons that steps would be taken to come to terms with the Boers, and these expressions of his intentions were promptly telegraphed to Africa, and were in the hands of the Boer leaders ; so that at every turn Sir Evelyn Wood found himself handicapped by the knowledge which his enemy possessed of the distinct instructions sent to him from home.   Distasteful as it must have been to carry out this policy, yet as a soldier he obeyed his orders to the letter.   Having come to terms for an armistice with General Joubert which was prolonged from time to time, he arranged for meetings with President Kruger, General Joubert, and Pretorius, who formed a triumvirate appointed by the rebellious Boers to represent them, with the view to drawing up conditions of peace.

On March 12, 1881, the Earl of Kimberley telegraphed to Major-General Sir Evelyn Wood, as follows

" Inform Boer leaders that if Boers will undertake to desist from armed opposition, and disperse to their homes, we are prepared to name the following as Commission :—Sir H. Robinson, Chief Justice de Villiers, and yourself.   President Brand would be asked to be present at proceedings as representing friendly State.   Commission would be authorised to consider following points :—Complete self-government under British suzerainty, with British resident at Pretoria, and provisions for protection of native interests, and as to frontier affairs.   Control over relations with foreign Powers to be reserved."

Influenced by these instructions, Sir E. Wood arranged for a meeting with the Boer leaders, and accordingly an interview took place on March 16, under Laings Nek, at which were present, General Sir Evelyn Wood and his staff, President Kruger and Messrs. Pretorius, P. Joubert, Jorissen, C. Joubert,

J. Mare and Dirk Uys. At this interview, President Kruger declared he was prepared to accept the terms of peace on the conditions of Lord Kimberley's telegram. He did so as follows :

" GENERAL WOOD. Do I now understand you to say that should Boer representatives be included as members of the Royal Commission you would accept the terms proposed in yesterday's communication as a basis of peace, bearing in mind that this implies immediate dispersion ?

" MR. KRUGER. Yes. I am prepared to accept terms of peace on the conditions mentioned in the communication of yesterday. I expect the British forces to withdraw from the Transvaal. Lord Kimberley in his telegram gives me my rights. I accept the telegram. There are minor details to be settled by the Commission —*e.g.*, boundaries, etc."

Later on President Kruger stated, " I accept suzerainty as explained by General Wood."

The definition being :

" Suzerainty means : That the country has entire self-government as regards its own interior affairs, but that it cannot take action against or with an outside power without the permission of the suzerain."

It is amusing and instructive also to find how at this interview the calm sagacious soldier understood those clever subterfuges which have made President Kruger famous as a diplomatist, to the discomfiture of most of our so-called statesmen.

As an illustration the following little passage of arms is, to my mind, particularly *à propos :*

"MR. KRUGER. The reason I wish to insist on withdrawal of your troops is, that if it be not done the people will be suspicious. If withdrawn, the labours of the Commission will be facilitated and the people would be grateful.

"GENERAL WOOD. *I should prefer a direct answer to my question rather than a contingent promise of gratitude.*"

Owing to the inclement weather and the non-arrival of President Brand, of the Orange Free State, the armistice was prolonged to March 21, and on that day a meeting took place between Sir Evelyn Wood, the delegates already mentioned, and Mr. Brand, who was present as the friend of both sides. This meeting is historical and one memorable in the annals of the Transvaal, as then the terms of peace were arranged and the principles laid down for the convention, which was subsequently signed. After having been explained to and accepted by the leaders of the disaffected Boers, Mr. Kruger suggested that the Act of Treaty should be drawn up. General Wood proposed to draft this in the first instance with Messrs. Kruger, Pretorius and Joubert. A draft was accordingly made and marked "B."

This agreement is of such vital importance, and so essential to estimate properly not only the position at the time of the armed Boer opposition, but also of the written instructions of Her Majesty's Government and of its policy, that I have decided to insert at this stage an exact copy of the document.*

"B.

"Result of a meeting at O'Neil's Farm on the 21st March 1881. Present: Sir Evelyn Wood, Majors Clarke and Fraser, Lieutenant Hamilton and Mr. T. Cropper, A.D.C.'s, on the one hand; Messrs. Kruger, Pretorius, P. Joubert, Jorissen, Dirk Uys, Maré C. Joubert, on the other hand.

"At the meetings of the 6th, 14th, and 16th of March 1881, between Sir E. Wood and the Boer leaders, it was agreed that an armistice be entered upon, and the Boer leaders subsequently accepted, in general, the conditions laid down in Lord Kimberley's telegrams of the 8th and 12th March, as communicated to them by Sir E. Wood, except on two points, viz.: (1) direct representation on the Commission, and (2) the expression of a hope that the English garrison in the Transvaal should withdraw when they dispersed. In their desire for peace the Boer representatives have since abandoned these two points.

"It is therefore agreed as follows :

"Schedule 1.—I, Sir Evelyn Wood, admit the Boer leaders, Messrs. Kruger, Pretorius, Joubert, and others who have been present at these meetings, as duly representing the people of the Transvaal, now in arms.

"Schedule 2.—We, Kruger, Pretorius, and Joubert declare our readiness to accept the suzerainty of the reigning Sovereign of Great Britain and Ireland,

* See Blue Book, C 3114, p. 55.

according to the explanation given by Sir E. Wood, as noted in the minutes of the meeting of the 16th March. We also agree to recognise a British Resident at the future capital of the Government, with such functions as the British Government may decide on the recommendations of the Royal Commission.

"We also agree to leave to the Commission the consideration of provision for the protection of native interests, and as to frontier affairs, that control of relations with foreign powers should be reserved to the Suzerain.

"Schedule 3.—I, Sir Evelyn Wood, acknowledge the right of the Transvaal people to complete self-government, subject to suzerain rights.

"Schedule 4.—We, Kruger, Pretorius, and Joubert, will gladly co-operate with Her Majesty's Government in bringing to justice those who have committed, or are directly responsible for, acts contrary to civilised warfare.

"Schedule 5.—I, Sir Evelyn Wood, in the event of the position on the Laings Nek being abandoned by the Boers, and of the latter dispersing to their homes, declare on the part of Her Majesty's Government that I will not take possession of that position, nor follow them up with troops, nor send ammunition into the Transvaal."

"At a meeting on March 18, a telegram from Lord Kimberley, dated 17th, was handed to the Boer representatives, being an answer to Sir E. Wood's telegram of the 16th, embodying the points raised by them on that day."

"Schedule 6.—The Boer leaders accept the terms offered in the telegram of the 17th. They declare, 'We trust to the British Government to give to us complete self-government as soon as possible, and at latest within six months, it being understood that no civil action shall be entertained in respect of proceedings taken during or in reference to this war, and equally no action be entertained in respect of taxation until the government be accorded. We further trust that if the Royal Commission considers any separation of land to the east of the 30th degree of longitude to be necessary, such Commission will not recommend the separation of more land than is necessary, for the purposes of the English policy as indicated in the telegram of March 17th.

"Schedule 7.—I, Sir E. Wood, do engage, on behalf of the British Government, that the Royal Commission shall meet at the earliest possible date, and that the government of the country shall be handed over within six months from this date.

"Schedule 8.—Under these circumstances, we, Kruger, Joubert, and Pretorius, engage on behalf of the Boers in arms, to disperse our forces at once, and to await the settlement of all pending questions referred to the Royal Commission; on the completion of the labours of which the country will enter on the promised self-government.

"Schedule 9.—We, Kruger, Joubert, and Pretorius, engage on behalf of the Boers, to restore all British property, now in possession of the Boer authorities, captured during the war, and Sir E. Wood undertakes to restore all property of the Boers now in possession

of the British Government, captured during the war, or
taken over from the Republic at the time of annexation.
The exchange to take place when the self-government
is finally accorded.

"(Signed)   EVELYN WOOD, Major-General,
                    "*Deputy High Commissioner.*
           "S. P. KRUGER.
           "H. W. PRETORIUS
           "P. J. JOUBERT."

This agreement speaks for itself.   It demonstrates conclusively what the Boer leaders of the armed opposition
accepted as binding on them in the future.   It is the
standard by which we must judge the convention, it
was the guide and chart of the Royal Commissioners
who were subsequently appointed.   The entire negotiations, so ably carried out by Sir Evelyn Wood with
great diplomatic skill and with soldierly firmness, were
approved and promptly ratified by Mr. Gladstone's
Cabinet; and the three Royal Commissioners, Sir
Hercules Robinson, High Commissioner for South
Africa, Sir Evelyn Wood, Commander of the forces in
Natal and the Transvaal, and Sir John Henry de
Villiers, Chief Justice of the Cape of Good Hope, were
duly appointed to be "Commissioners to inquire into
and report upon all matters relating to the future settlement of the Transvaal."

It follows then, as a natural consequence, that instructions from the Home Government should be sent to
these commissioners, and hence we find on March 31,
1881, the Earl of Kimberley instructed Sir Hercules
Robinson and his associates at great length as to the
duties to be performed by them, as to the conditions

they should impose, and as to the guarantees for the due performance of those conditions which had to be given by Her Majesty, as suzerain. A perusal of these instructions acquaints us with the fact that Mr. Gladstone's Cabinet adhered mainly to the demands imposed on, and agreed to by, the Boer leaders on March 21, but one important item therein absolutely fettered and hampered at least two of the Commissioners throughout their discussions with Mr. Kruger and his friends. ' Nothing demonstrated so plainly the state of abject flabbiness into which the Home Government had sunk as that statement set forth by Lord Kimberley for the guidance of the Royal Commissioners. Here it is:

"With regard to the Lydenburg district apart from New Scotland, the arguments in favour of maintaining British rule over it are that the population is stated to contain an increasing British element, principally at the Gold Fields; that the native population vastly out-number the white inhabitants, being estimated at 123,300 as compared with 1578; and that having subdued Sikukuni's tribe, which occupies an important part of the district, we are under peculiar obligations to make provision for its fair treatment.

"On the other hand the Lydenburg district could scarcely be annexed to Natal, and as a separate British Province it would form an inconvenient narrow strip of territory which would probably, for some time to come, not pay its own expenses. *Lastly, Her Majesty's Government are averse, on general grounds of policy, to the extension of British Territory in South Africa:*

" A most important consideration will be the wishes of the settlers themselves, and you will be careful to ascertain in the fullest manner whether they would willingly accept the continuance of British rule, if it should be determined to retain any of the territory to which I have referred."

When Lord Kimberley, as Colonial Secretary, despatched these instructions to the Royal Commissioners, there had been no intention either expressed or implied to extend the area of British territory in South Africa. But Her Majesty's Government had at many times contracted obligations towards those Kaffir tribes who had been conquered by us and who had come under our protection, and the fulfilment of these was binding on us.

Sekukuni was an independent chief when the Boers attacked him. Cetewayo's territory had never formed a portion of the Republic, neither had the Swazi country ever been subject to Boer control; moreover, the Triumvirate in their negotiations with Sir Evelyn Wood had practically agreed to our right to fix the boundaries necessary to protect our colonists, and to carry out our pledges to the natives.

What justification or reason, then, had Lord Kimberley for sending this Little Englander declaration of policy to the Commissioners ? It was not to be supposed for a moment that they would attempt to extend the Empire by acquiring new territory for the Crown. No, the difficulty they had to get over was how to surrender with a grace, territory which different British Cabinets, and their representative officers, had declared would always form an integral part of Her Majesty's dominions.

It was a question of scuttle, not of extension, and solemn pledges made to both white men and natives were *ipso facto* to be broken.

Why then, may we ask, did Lord Kimberley further perplex the minds of his Commissioners with the disturbing fear that if they fixed certain boundaries they would be acting contrary to the policy of the Government?

To his honour be it recorded, one of the three Commissioners, Sir Evelyn Wood, had the courage of his convictions, and this statement of policy did not cause him to swerve from the path of duty which had been already marked out for him, not only by Mr. Gladstone's and Lord Kimberley's predecessors, but by themselves. He had the manliness to dissent from his colleagues, and his reasons are set out in his special report, an extract from which I append.*

"2. With reference to the territorial question, Sir Evelyn Wood is unable to concur with his colleagues in the arguments which led them to recommend the abandonment of the scheme of separation of territory agreed to at Laing's Nek. Paragraphs 44 to 53 of this Report give the arguments of the Boer leaders against the separation of any territory east of the 30th degree of longitude.

"These objections must have been just as evident to the leaders, when treating with Sir Evelyn Wood at Laing's Nek, as when treating with the Commission at Newcastle. At Laing's Nek they acquiesced in the

* Book Book, C 3114.

principle of separation of territory; that they did so is, Sir Evelyn Wood thinks, a proof that they preferred peace, with the proposed separation, to a continuance of war.

" To contend afterwards that the Royal Commission ought not to decide contrary to the wishes of the Boers, because such decision might not be accepted, is to deny to the Commission the very power of decision that it was agreed should be left in its hands.

" In paragraphs 53 and 54 the majority of the Commission hold that sentiment was the mainspring of the late outbreak, and imply that none of the peace stipulations antagonistic to this feeling can be enforced without detriment to the permanent tranquillity of the country. Sir Evelyn Wood cannot concur with even the premises of his colleagues, and he is convinced the approximate cause of the late outbreak was a general and rooted aversion to taxation.

" His colleagues appear to have received the statements of the leaders as expressing the feelings of their followers. In Sir Evelyn Wood's opinion the views of the Triumvirate should have been accepted with reserve; and he could not attach the same value that the majority of the Commission did to the Leaders' account of Boer sentiments. As it was, his colleagues arrived at their conclusions on this question in Newcastle before the Commission had entered the Transvaal, and practically before they had any opportunity of learning the wishes of the inhabitants, except through the mouths of the leaders.

" As Sir Evelyn Wood cannot accept the conclusions of his colleagues, based on the arguments of the Boers,

E

still less can he accept those they have arrived at in paragraphs 56 and 57, on the aspect of the native question. It is argued that by concessions to the Boers on the territorial question the Commission would obtain large powers for the British Resident, and also gain the consent of the Boers to conditions not contained in the peace agreement, viz. :

"The creation of a native location Commission, the right of veto on native legislation, and the settlement of the disputed boundary of the Keate Award territory, all of which will, the majority of the Commission think, form the best guarantees for the protection of all native interests.

"Schedule 2 of the agreement of the 21st March, 1881, left to the Commission to define, and to the British Government to determine, what powers should be assigned to the Resident, and what provision should be made for the protection of native interests, while Schedule 3 made complete self-government *subject to suzerain rights.*

"It is not apparent to Sir Evelyn Wood that in the Convention any powers greater than those justified by the peace agreement have been so assigned to the Resident, and the creation of a Native Location Commission, the power of veto on native legislation, and the settlement of the Keate Award question, appear to him to be matters so directly affecting native interests, as to be entirely within the scope of the agreement of the 21st March ; however, be this as it may, he cannot believe that any power the Government or the Resident may derive from the Convention will prove as beneficial to the natives as would the existence of

British rule eastward of the 30th degree of longitude.

"It is admitted that all the eastern natives would prefer the retention of British rule in this country, and also, that it would benefit them ; it is, however, argued that these are the natives best able to protect themselves.

"To a certain degree this is correct, but we have recently destroyed the military power of the Zulu nation and have disarmed the people.

"In the interests of the Transvaal, but at England's expense, we subdued Sikukuni, and we have checked the acquisition of firearms by all natives.

"Sir Evelyn Wood maintains, therefore, that the eastern tribes are not so capable of defence as to be independent of our protection ; and while admitting they are not so defenceless as are those on the western border of the Transvaal, he submits that the arguments of his colleagues prove more conclusively the importance of protecting the natives on the west than the desirability of withdrawing protection from those on the east side of the Transvaal.

"Sir Evelyn Wood's colleagues admit the desirability of retaining the eastern territory under British rule, and the substantial benefit to the natives living therein and to the eastward of it ; but they argue that those in the west, who, by their position, are unavoidably excluded from our protection, would have suffered loss by missing those favourable conditions which have been secured to them by the Convention. The value of the said conditions must be a matter of opinion until tested by time, and the necessity for

making concessions to obtain them is not, Sir Evelyn
Wood submits, apparent; but whichever may be
the more accurate view, in summing up numeri-
cally the interests concerned, the question cannot be
confined to those named, but should be considered
to extend indirectly to all the natives in South-east
Africa.

"Sir Evelyn Wood agrees with his colleagues in
thinking that the grounds for retaining the country east
of the Drakensberg are less cogent than those for
retaining the whole territory east of the 30th degree,
and he admits that the relatively small number of the
Transvaal natives east of the Drakensberg does not
alone justify the proposed rectification of the boundaries, but he cannot follow his colleagues in the rest
of their argument, and thinks that, while studying how
best to balance the interests of Boers and natives, they
have overlooked, what was to him the most important
factor in the question, viz., the interests of the English
colonies in South Africa. The proposal for a separation
of territory proceeded from Her Majesty's Government.
In the month of March, when the negotiations at Laing's
Nek were approaching completion, Sir Evelyn Wood
submitted to the Secretary of State for the Colonies
what he considered would be (for British and native
interests) the most suitable boundaries for the Transvaal in case we left it.

"The Commission being opposed to the retention of
the territory lying to the eastward of the 30th degree
of longitude, Sir Evelyn Wood suggested as a compromise the retention of the district which lies to the
east of the Drakensberg; but it was far less in the

interests of its native population that the smaller measure was suggested, than for the sake of tranquillity in Swaziland, Zululand, and Natal. His colleagues have balanced the eastern and western native question by a comparison of numbers, but a glance at the map will show how very much more important it is to our Colonies to have quiet on the eastern than on the western borders. Separated as we now shall be by the Transvaal from the eastern natives it will be impossible for us to exercise over them the influence for peace due to our paramount position in the country.

"It is from this cause, he thinks, trouble to England may arise, and this is the consideration which has led him to dissent from his colleagues on the territorial question."

But I desire to do Lord Kimberley justice, and perhaps the doctrine that a Government is entitled to change its policy by its own volition regardless of its obligations had become matured in his mind. To make myself perfectly clear, I assume that his views on the Transvaal situation were at that period identical with those he holds to-day *quâ* Turkey, and which he enunciated a few weeks ago at Norwich.

He then said :

" My present view is that whatever treaty may have been concluded in 1856, it is idle to say that the British policy has now to be bound by it as if it was a treaty concluded yesterday. It is not a treaty which can bind us to such a degree that, if we think another policy is required, we are not to be allowed to change our policy."

Now a treaty may be described as an instrument embodying stipulated conditions under which the parties affected have agreed they can live in peaceful accord with each other. Again, a treaty is generally the natural consequence of a dispute or disagreement which may or may not have been settled after armed conflict.

At any rate, it represents the convictions and intentions of the parties interested in the settlement of such disputes. It is the most solemn form of contract known to mankind, regulating not simply the interests of individuals, but the present and future welfare of nations.

Infractions and infringements are only to be dealt with in two ways : First, by moral suasion ; secondly, by force of arms. In the latter event the treaty no longer exists.

No statute of limitations governs a treaty. It is in force so long as the parties abide by its conditions, and the withdrawal from it, or wilful infraction of any of its provisions, by one party to it, constitutes no reason why the other should acquiesce in this act of repudiation or should change the policy which had been evolved from the mature deliberations of the wise and prudent men at the head of the nations interested.

In other words, violation of a treaty by one party affords no reason for a change of policy by the other. On the contrary, such violation should operate as a stimulus to maintain manfully the policy which originates the treaty itself.

Let us now apply Lord Kimberley's dictum at Norwich to the situation in 1881. The Boers having violated the terms of the Sand River Treaty of 1852 " British policy was no longer to be bound by it as if it was a treaty concluded yesterday," and therefore a change of policy to his mind was necessary. But even so, I do not see how this doctrine can be applicable to the position he had then to confront, because only three years before we had been compelled to annex the Transvaal to save our colonists and the Boers themselves, from the consequences of their impotence, and to prevent bloodshed throughout South Africa.

But here we have the key-note to all the events which subsequently transpired in 1884, and to the contempt for the conventions always manifested by the Boers. Not only did Lord Kimberley's declaration of policy prejudice and affect the minds of two of the Commissioners when dealing with the apportionment of territory, but astute Hollanders, ever at the elbow of these illiterate though cunning Boers, learnt from this despatch, when published and laid before Parliament, this miserable history of weakness. And more, from our Blue Books they became rightly convinced, between 1881 and 1884, that only a little pressure was required to be put on the men who were in office prior to the Convention to gain all that they desired ; that is to say, the abrogation of the leading principles which, in the Convention of 1881, Mr. Gladstone's Cabinet had guaranteed in the name of Her Majesty as sacred and binding.

Englishmen, and indeed men of every nationality who

have taken up their abode in the Transvaal, or who have invested their money in that country, must feel profoundly thankful that at this hour there is a reasonable hope that British policy will not be conducted on such weathercock principles.

And now let us see what the Convention of 1881 comprised.

CHAPTER IV

CONVENTION OF 1881

NEVER during the long reign of the Queen has this realm been placed before the world in such a humiliating light by responsible advisers of the Crown as in its relations with the Transvaal State. Her Majesty's ministers in 1880 had before them the history of our transactions with the Boers extending over long years; for in despatches, reports and statements, trustworthy officials on the spot had repeatedly furnished unimpeachable evidence not only of the Boers' incapacity for rule, but also of their utter disregard of all treaties or conventions. Moreover, all the circumstances which had impelled the Crown to annex the Republic and our recent wars with Sekukuni and Cetewayo, which arose out of Boer impotence and threatened at one time to turn South Africa into a vast charnel-house, were within their immediate ken.

Nevertheless, the pledges of different Cabinets were broken, solemn promises made by high officials set aside, and the rights of those persons who, placing reliance on such pledges and promises, had taken up their abode and invested their money in the country, were trampled on by Mr. Gladstone and his Ministers under the flimsy cloak of sympathy with an oppressed race struggling for liberty.

Lest there should be any misapprehension as to the promises which had been made to the inhabitants of the Transvaal State, or that Her Majesty's Government were ignorant of them, I will quote from a memorial presented to the Royal Commissioners on May 20, 1881,* and from a petition addressed to the House of Commons by the loyal inhabitants of the Transvaal.†

" Nor is it necessary to dilate upon the panic which has taken place since the peace, and which has been made public through the press. The Committee of Loyal Inhabitants is informed that the banks intend leaving, and all credit is suspended. Some part of the panic may be due to temporary excitement, but the want of confidence must be permanent, as the Boers have no money, and no one will lend them any. English capitalists certainly will not, nor are the Hollanders, busy as they have been in fanning the agitation which has helped towards the peace, likely to spend much money in the country after the experience they have had of the Delagoa Bay railway scheme. It cannot be long before the State is again insolvent, unless it is helped from without ; and the circumstances under which the Boer Government is likely to be carried on, judging from past experience, will not invite capital into it. Hence there will necessarily follow a lasting depreciation of the value of property, and the fears of the claimants, expressed in some of the affidavits, that

* See Blue Book C 3114, pp. 179 and 180.
† See Blue Book C 3114, pp. 183 and 184.

the depreciation will be at least 50 per cent. of the value, are certainly not beyond the mark.

"But there is another aspect at which to look at the question. Not only is there a contract for compensation to be implied from the acts of the British Government, but there are promises and pledges, amounting to an 'express warranty,' contained in speeches and in proclamations, and made in the most solemn and authoritative manner, by Prime Ministers, by colonial secretaries, by governors, and by administrators, and in fact by almost every person who has had right or authority to bind the English Government since the annexation. It is not necessary to quote every proclamation and every speech, as their general effect is matter of common knowledge, and cannot be unknown to your Excellencies. Sir Theophilus Shepstone, Sir Garnet Wolseley, Sir Bartle Frere and Sir Owen Lanyon, have all declared repeatedly that the country could not be given back. Sir Garnet Wolseley used the remarkable expression more than once that the Transvaal would remain British territory as long as the sun shone; and it will be seen by reference to the affidavits that this emphatic declaration from so high an authority was the immediate and direct cause of several persons investing money in landed property in the Transvaal. But it was not only governors and administrators who gave utterance to such declarations; Earl Beaconsfield, when at the head of affairs in England, made statements to the same effect, as also did Lord Carnarvon, then the Colonial Secretary, and his successor in office, Sir Michael Hicks-Beach. The latter, in a letter to Sir Owen Lanyon announcing the establishment of a Provisional Government, dated the 20th November 1879, and published in the *Government Gazette* of the 8th January 1880, uses such remarkable words that we must quote them at length. He says :

"'It would not be possible, and if possible, it would be injurious to the country, to re-establish the form of government which existed before the 12th April, 1877. The interests of the large native population, who now (with the exception of Sikukuni and those associated with him) are quiet and contented; of the European settlers, who have acquired property in the Province, *in the full belief* that the annexation will be maintained ; and of the peaceful and industrious residents in and about Pretoria, and other centres of population, in whose hands is nearly all the commerce of the country, *have apparently been entirely disregarded* by those who would deprive them of the advantages which they desire to retain under the authority of the Crown.'

"It is perhaps unnecessary to explain that the concluding words do not refer to the British Government, but to the Boer agitators.

"The pledges of the Beaconsfield Government were endorsed by Mr. Gladstone, on his taking office, in a special manner in May 1880, and again on the outbreak of the war ; and Lord Kimberley, the present Secretary of State for the Colonies, stated publicly, and his statement was, we believe, published in the *Government Gazette*, that under *no* circumstances could Her Majesty's dominion over the Transvaal be relinquished."

" To the Honourable the Commons of the United Kingdom of Great Britain and Ireland in Parliament
assembled.

" The humble Petition of the Loyal Inhabitants of the
Transvaal.

" Sheweth :

That the country now known as the Transvaal
was forcibly taken possession of, in or about the year
1836, by emigrant Boers from the Cape Colony, who
were at the time British subjects.

" That the natives, to whom the country then
belonged, were either driven out of the country, or
reduced to a state of subjection or servitude.

" That by the Sand River Convention in 1852, the
emigrants were permitted by the British Government
to establish themselves as an independent Republic,
subject to certain conditions.

" That from the year 1852 up to the year 1877 the
country remained subject to a Boer Republican
Government, when the British Government exercised
its dormant authority, and annexed it to England.

" That on repeated occasions since the annexation,
successive Governors of the Transvaal have given
pledges by proclamation and by word of mouth that the
country would remain British territory, and would not
be restored to the Boers, and that in particular by a
proclamation, dated October 7th, 1879, Sir Garnet
Wolseley stated that, in order to remove any doubt as
to the maintenance of British authority, he made it
known that the Transvaal would continue to be an
integral portion of Her Majesty's dominions, and on

more than one occasion he stated that the Transvaal would remain British territory as long as the sun shone.

" That Mr. Gladstone, who was then Prime Minister of England, stated in reply to a memorial addressed to him by the loyal inhabitants of Pretoria about May 1880, that he had already informed the Boer representatives, who had addressed him, that the annexation could not be rescinded, endorsing the pledges and declared policy of Earl Beaconsfield, his predecessor in office ; and that Lord Kimberley, the Secretary of State for the Colonies, in a telegram to Sir Owen Lanyon, the Administrator of the Province, and in order to allay doubts which had arisen in consequence of the continued agitation of the Boers, said, that under no circumstances could Her Majesty's dominion over the Transvaal be relinquished.

" That inasmuch as Her Majesty's Government exercised the supreme control of the affairs of the Province, and were cognisant of the whole question in all its bearings from the commencement, including the position taken by Boer agitators during the later part of the period in question, and that they had notwithstanding declared so repeatedly and in such unmistakable terms that the annexation would never be rescinded, and especially so lately as last year, your petitioners were justified in concluding that the British nation had irrevocably and after the utmost deliberation determined that under *all* circumstances the Transvaal should remain under British rule.

" That firmly relying upon these solemn pledges, and confiding in the steadfastness of purpose and fidelity to obligations which have up to the time of the present ill-advised treaty made the name of England respected by civilised and savage nations alike, and fully believing that her ancient traditions would never permit her to break her word, numbers of British subjects and European immigrants settled in the country with a view of making it their home, and invested largely in land and property, on the strength of the security and protection afforded by British rule.

" That the value of property increased at least three-fold during the English occupation, and that the increase progressed in a ratio correspondent with the reliance placed on the promises of English officials. Indeed, some of your petitioners are prepared to state, on oath if required, that they invested money immediately after or in direct consequence of a statement made by a Governor of the Transvaal or a Minister of the British Crown.

" That the towns are almost exclusively inhabited by loyal subjects, and English farmers and traders are scattered all over the country.

" That the inhabitants of European or Cape extraction, a large proportion of whom have settled in the country since the English occupation, form at the lowest estimate one in seven of the white population, and are in the possession of from one-third to one-half of the property, exclusive of Crown Lands. The total white population is not more than 40,000, while the natives are estimated at about 700,000. In Pretoria alone during the late war 4300 people, not including the military, took shelter in the camp from the Boers, and were rationed by the Government.

"That a large number of the Boer population, who had learned to appreciate the advantages of a settled rule, refused to fight against the British during the late war, and took refuge, some in laagers of their own and others among the natives.   The unexpected termination of the war presses with peculiar hardness on these loyal Boers, as it renders it impossible for them to return in safety to their homes, and has practically ruined them as a reward for their loyalty and trust in the honour of England."

In face of the above facts, even Mr. Gladstone and his Cabinet could not for very shame altogether repudiate the acts of their predecessors as well as their own plighted word, and one cannot help concluding that either he and his colleagues were overwhelmed by a wave of moral cowardice, such as never before overtook any British Ministry, or were feverishly anxious to justify themselves to their constituents and to the country at large so as to retain office.

For even whilst indulging in a parade of mock sentiment, they were secretly abasing themselves before the Boers, as we learn from Lord Kimberley's telegrams to Sir George Colley and Sir Evelyn Wood, and later, on the death of the former, they set aside the advice of his military successor on the spot, and from day to day wailingly ordered him to truckle to the Boer leaders, in order to obtain their consent to terms of peace.

Nor could Mr. Gladstone's Cabinet ignore the obligations entailed on them by the annexation, for they were driven to confront the altered circumstances which had arisen since April 1877.   It was this, doubtless, which

led Mr. Gladstone himself, before he assumed the garb
of sentiment, to make the statement in 1880 already
recorded.   And however anxious, a little later on, he
and his Ministers might have personally been to eat the
leek, the large majority of Englishmen at home were
not so frightened as to forget that the Crown had
duties to both loyal Boers and other inhabitants
who had settled in the country after its annexation.
Further, the obligations towards the large native
population under our protection or control had to be
taken into account, and, that even when making a
humiliating peace, some regard for Imperial pledges
and authority had to be exhibited.   Therefore, although
Mr. Gladstone's Cabinet, through Lord Kimberley, had
fettered their own Commissioners by the statement
that " Her Majesty's Government were averse on
general grounds of policy to the extension of British
territory in South Africa," we must assume that,
setting aside the question of territorial acquisition, all
other conditions embraced in their instructions clearly
showed the length to which Mr. Gladstone and his
colleagues could go in any settlement.

For future guidance, then, let us examine the nature
of Lord Kimberley's instructions.   I append below
those most pertinent to our present consideration—the
full text will be found in the Appendix.

" Instructions.

"The Right Hon. the EARL OF KIMBERLEY to
Sir HERCULES ROBINSON, G.C.M.G.

" It may be desirable that the Commission should, in
the first instance, address itself to the principal points

F

referred to in the general terms of settlement, agreed to by Sir E. Wood with the Boer leaders, a summary of which is contained in his telegram to me of March 21st,* and, to some extent, further explained in subsequent telegraphic correspondence. I may recapitulate them, as follows :

"*The Transvaal State is to enjoy complete self-government under the suzerainty of the Queen; the control of its relations with foreign Powers being reserved to the British Government.*

"*A British Resident may be appointed at the capital of the Transvaal State, with such functions as Her Majesty's Government may determine on the recommendation of the Commission.*

"*The Commission is to consider provisions for the protection of native interests.*

"The Commission is further to consider whether any portion, within certain limits, mentioned in my telegram to Sir E. Wood, of March 17th,† should be severed from the country now included in the Transvaal Province.

"There is to be no molestation for political opinion either way, and a complete amnesty is to be accorded to all who have taken part in the present war, excepting only persons who have committed, or are directly responsible for, acts contrary to the rules of civilised warfare.

"Immunity from civil process is guaranteed to the Boer leaders, individually and collectively, for acts done in reference to the war until self-government is accorded, and the question of compensation to either

* No. 123 of (C 2837) March 1881.
† No. 115 of (C 2837) March 1881.

side, for acts not justified by necessities of war, is remitted to the Commission to judge what acts were justified.

"Besides these principal points there are some other matters referred to in the agreement entered into by Sir E. Wood, as reported in his telegrams to me, and there are further points not mentioned by him, which will have to be provided for in the final settlement. Of the latter the most important are the determination of a boundary line in the territory known as the Keate award, the payment of the public debt of the province, and the recognition of all lawful acts done by the Government during the British occupation. I will deal in order with the various points to which I have referred.

"Entire freedom of action will be accorded to the Transvaal Government so far as is not inconsistent with the rights expressly reserved to the suzerain Power. The term suzerainty has been chosen as most conveniently describing superiority over a State possessing independent rights of government subject to reservations with reference to certain specified matters.

"*The most material of these reserved rights is the control of the external relations of the future Transvaal State, which will be vested in the British Government, including, of course, the conclusion of treaties and the conduct of diplomatic intercourse with foreign Powers.*

"*As regards communication with foreign Governments, it will probably be found most convenient that the Transvaal Government should correspond on such matters with Her Majesty's Government through the Resident and the High Commissioner.*

" There remains, for consideration under this head, the manner in which the relations with the independent native tribes beyond the frontier should be conducted. The general superintendence of these relations would seem naturally to fall within the functions of the British Resident under the direction of the High Commissioner. It will be for the Royal Commissioners, after examination of the whole question, to recommend what should be the precise limits of the powers assigned to the Resident in regard to this important matter. You will bear in mind that the objects to be aimed at are to preserve the peace of the frontier, and to maintain a course of policy conducive generally to the interest and tranquillity of the whole of South Africa, and that Her Majesty's Government have no desire to interfere with the local administration beyond what may be indispensable for the furtherance of these objects."

Thus the terms of settlement agreed on between Sir Evelyn Wood and the Boer leaders on March 21 were to form the basis of any definitive understanding. Now, the first stipulation laid down was that Her Majesty as suzerain should control all the foreign relations of the State for all time, even to the extent that it could have no intercourse with outside Powers save through British diplomatic officials. In every sense of the word the new State was to be a vassal of the Crown, and not an independent sovereign power. Then, as paramount authority, Her Majesty would guarantee to all inhabitants of the new State complete self-government *under Her suzerainty*, and the enjoyment of all civil rights to every person then resident in the country, as well as to those who should hereafter take up their abode therein, subject to defined conditions.

Especial care was to be taken for the proper provision of native interests, and Her Majesty's own Resident Officer was to be charged with their protection.

Now the terms demanded, and already generally acceded to on March 21, are set forth in this misnamed Convention of 1881. I say misnamed, because a convention or treaty is usually an agreement arrived at between two or more independent States. In this instance it was a guarantee by Her Majesty that a vassal State should be accorded complete self-government subject to conditions imposed by her as suzerain.

This guarantee was to extend to all the inhabitants of the country, and if a section of them, to the detriment of others, wilfully broke the conditions under which that guarantee had been given, all the other aggrieved parties could call on the suzerain to enforce the guarantee.

That this can be the only interpretation is clear from the document itself. Unlike any ordinary treaty or convention, it commences without preamble or recitals, and in bold and terse language declares what the suzerain accords to the inhabitants of the Transvaal State, subject[1] of course to their compliance with the terms thereinafter set forth.

It commences thus : *

" Her Majesty's Commissioners for the settlement of the Transvaal Territory, duly appointed as such by a Commission passed under the Royal Sign Manual and

* Blue Book C 1114, p 37.

Signet bearing date April 5, 1881, *do hereby undertake and guarantee on behalf of Her Majesty that, from and after the 8th day of August,* 1881, *complete self-government, subject to the suzerainty of Her Majesty, her heirs and successors, will be accorded to the inhabitants of the Transvaal Territory, upon the following terms and conditions, and subject to the following reservations and limitations."*

To appreciate the intention of the parties, as expressed in this document, we must remember that though Her Majesty's Commissioners discussed these conditions with men representing a section of the Transvaal community which had recently taken up arms, there were others to be considered whose lives, property and interests Her Majesty was bound to safeguard. These were :

(1) Loyal Boers.

(2) British Colonists, and foreigners who had settled mainly through, and after, the annexation ; and

(3) Native tribes.

Before the "Convention" was drafted, long conferences took place between the Commissioners and the Boer leaders, and every point which subsequently became one of the conditions set forth in the different articles of the Convention was carefully threshed out between them. The Boers in opposition then, beyond all others, were bound by these terms, conditions, limitations and reservations, inasmuch as they alone were admitted to discuss and accept the form, nature, and spirit of the Convention, to which they afterwards affixed their names. It is plain that Her Majesty's object was that all sections should become united, that all should enjoy equal rights and privileges, and thus cement relations with each other, founded on principles of equity and justice.   Hence, at the very outset, we find that the chief pledge Her Majesty gave was a guarantee of complete self-government to all the inhabitants of the Transvaal Territory, and not to those Boers alone who had recently been in arms against her authority.

Self-government naturally involves the right of each person to the franchise, subject to the restrictions or qualifications imposed by law, and as this right had such an important bearing on the mutual relations of the members of this mixed community, it is essential for us to inquire what qualification was needful at the time to enable a man to become a burgher, or to vote for members of the Volksraad.   A reference to the Blue Book shows that this question presented itself to the minds of the Commissioners, and that they were anxious to learn from the Boer leaders what was the position of a foreigner, or outlander, coming into the country under the Grondwet at the time of annexation. Mr. Kruger, as we gather from his explanation, was desirous of creating a good impression on the Commissioners, and he made distinct statements and promises which they undoubtedly believed, and accordingly, when framing their article, safeguarding to each person an equality of civil rights, they did so in the spirit and with the intent that no alteration should at any time be made in the law, by which an outsider might be hindered in acquiring the privileges of a burgher.   The following extracts from the discussion prior to the signing of the Convention are instructive.*

"Question 239. Sir H. Robinson.—Before annexation, had British subjects complete freedom of trade throughout the Transvaal; were they on the same footing as citizens?

"240. Mr. Kruger.—They were on the same footing as the burghers; there was not the slightest difference in accordance with the Sand River Convention.

"241. Sir H. Robinson.—I presume you will not object to that continuing?

"242. Mr. Kruger.—No, there will be equal protection for everybody.

"243. Sir E. Wood.—And equal privileges?

"244. Mr. Kruger.—We make no difference as far as burgher rights are concerned. There may perhaps be some slight difference in the case of a young person who has just come into the country.

"245.—There are no disabilities with regard to trade are there?

"246. Mr. Kruger.—No."

At page 53 of the same book we find that at a subsequent meeting Dr. Jorissen, in Mr. Kruger's presence, corrected Mr. Kruger's answer to Sir E. Wood.

"1037. Dr. Jorissen.—At No. 244 the question was: 'Is there any distinction in regard to the privileges or rights of Englishmen in the Transvaal?' and Mr. Kruger answered, 'No, there is no difference'; and then

* Blue Book C 3219, p. 24.

he added, 'there may be some slight difference in the case of a young person just coming into the country.' I wish to say that that might give rise to a wrong impression. What Mr. Kruger intended to convey was this : according to our law a new-comer has not his burgher rights immediately. The words young person do not refer to age, but to the time of residence in the Republic. According to our Grondwet (Constitution) you have to reside a year in the country.

"1038. Sir H. de Villiers.—Is the oath of allegiance required from a person, not being born in the Transvaal, coming to reside there, who claims burgher rights ?

"1039. Dr. Jorissen.—In the law relating to the franchise there is a stipulation for the oath of allegiance to be taken to the State.

"1040.—Then it is not every burgher who has a vote ; it is only the burghers who have taken the oath of allegiance that have a vote ?

"1041. Dr. Jorissen.—Yes, the last revision of that law was made in 1876."

Now enactments of the Volksraad, and the Boers' fundamental constitution, their Grondwet, must be taken as being within the cognisance of the parties at the time this Convention was signed, and therefore we are compelled to interpret the different articles embraced in the Convention according to the intention and knowledge of those who agreed to them. It is evident that the Boers conveyed to the minds of the Royal Commissioners that they were desirous to increase by every means possible the number of burghers, for in a previous despatch addressed to the Commissioners by the Triumvirate respecting the boundaries, they state that if certain steps were taken these "would prevent the much desired affiliation of the colonists of different nationalities throughout South Africa."

What then does this mean? Nothing short of the facts already contended for—that at that time, if the Boer leaders were sincere (which Her Majesty's Commissioners had every right to believe them to be) they desired, in order to benefit their country, and to make the nation more powerful, to give Burgher Rights under their laws existing before 1877, to persons of any nationality whatever, who might dwell within their borders. Her Majesty's Commissioners, on their side, not merely safeguarded the rights of the inhabitants, as well as those who might in future settle there, under Her Majesty's guarantee, from the 8th day of August 1881, to the enjoyment of complete self-government, but in the Convention they gave effect to the desire of the Boer leaders, as expressed by themselves.

There are other civil rights, however, besides the exercise of the franchise, as the Commissioners were aware, and, to protect each section of the community, they took every precaution to particularise and express in the terms and conditions what benefits the inhabitants of the country were to enjoy in common, under Her Majesty's guarantee of self-government to all.

For example, Article 12 of the Convention declares:

"That all persons holding property in the State on the 8th day of August 1881, will continue to enjoy the rights of property which they have enjoyed since the annexation. That no person who has remained loyal to Her Majesty during the recent hostilities shall suffer by reason of his loyalty, and that all persons will have full liberty to reside in the country, with enjoyment of all civil rights and protection for their persons and property."

Again, by Article 26 it was established :

"That all persons conforming to the laws of the Transvaal State will have full liberty to enter, travel, or reside in any part of the State, they will be entitled to possess or hire houses, manufactories, warehouses, shops and premises. They may carry on their commerce either in person or by any agents whom they may think fit to employ, they will not be subject in respect of their persons or property, or in respect of their commerce or industry to any tax, whether general or local, other than those which are, or may be, imposed on the Transvaal citizens."

But this is not all. To provide against any legislation to the detriment or injury of the rights of persons then resident, or to the rights of future comers into the land under the guarantee of Her Majesty, it was expressed in Article 3 of the said Convention that :

"Until altered by the Volksraad or other competent authority all laws, whether passed before or after the annexation of the Transvaal Territory to Her Majesty's dominions, shall, except in so far as they are inconsistent with or repugnant to the provisions of this Convention, be and remain in force in the said State in so far as they shall be applicable thereto : Provided that, in the future, enactments specially affecting the interests of natives shall have no force or effect in the said State without the consent of Her Majesty, her heirs or successors, first being obtained and signified through the British Resident : Provided further that in no case will the repeal or amendment of any laws which have been enacted since the annexation have a retrospective effect so as to invalidate any acts done or liabilities incurred by virtue of such laws."

It is evident, then, that all the parties were agreed that no law should be passed which would alter or rescind those then in force, relating to rights *inter se*. Such alterations if made would be repugnant to the provisions of the Convention, and, therefore, until a Volksraad, thoroughly representative of the inhabitants, was summoned all laws then in existence were to be maintained. And this is natural, for until a Volksraad properly constituted were elected, no change could be legally made in the Grondwet, and further, that in the case of natives, the inhabitants of the country through their Volksraad could pass no enactments interfering with, or affecting, native interests without the consent of Her Majesty being first obtained and signified through the British Resident.

Great stress, as we have seen, was laid on the appointment of a British Resident to represent the suzerain, nor was this desire confined to Her Majesty's Ministers. The Boer leaders, when they wanted to hoodwink Her

Majesty's Commissioners on the eastern boundary question, pointed out to them what a blessing such an appointment would confer on the Boers themselves. Read by the light of what transpired later, this bit of hypocrisy must be regarded as a gem.*

"The constant presence in the capital of the country of Her Majesty's representative, his prestige as such, his constant counsel and advice, will, if necessary, remove every difficulty which may arise, but which we as honourable men are not able to foresee. Experience has taught us that the very absence of such a high placed diplomatic person in our Republic has created the greatest misunderstanding, which gave cause to the annexation."

Those worthies who signed the above statement were S. P. Kruger, M. W. Pretorius, P. J. Joubert, E. Jorissen, J. S. Joubert.

There is no article of this "Convention" more explicit or more emphatic than Article 2, which declares the rights Her Majesty reserves, as paramount power, over her vassals.

"Article 2.—Her Majesty reserves to herself, her heirs and successors, (a) the right from time to time to appoint a British Resident in and for the said State, with such duties and functions as are herein-after defined ; (b) the right to move troops through the said State in time of war, or in case of the apprehension of immediate war between the Suzerain Power and any

* May 11, 1881. Despatch from Boer leaders, C 3114, p 63.

Foreign State or Native Tribe in South Africa ; and
(c) the control of the external relations of the said State,
including the conclusion of treaties and the conduct of
diplomatic intercourse with Foreign Powers, such intercourse to be carried on through Her Majesty's diplomatic
and consular officers abroad."

Her Majesty's first reservation then was "the right
from time to time to appoint a British Resident in and
for the said State, with such duties and functions as
are herein-after defined," and in Article 18 those duties
and functions are set out in the plainest manner :

"Article 18. The following will be the duties and
functions of the British Resident :—Sub-section 1.   He
will perform duties and functions analogous to those
discharged by a Chargé d'Affaires and Consul-General.

"Sub-section 2. In regard to natives within the
Transvaal State he will (a) report to the High Commissioner, as representative of the Suzerain, as to the
working and observance of the provisions of this
Convention ; (b) report to the Transvaal authorities
any cases of ill-treatment of natives or attempts to
incite natives to rebellion that may come to his knowledge ; (c) use his influence with the natives in favour
of law and order ; and (d) generally perform such other
duties as are by this Convention entrusted to him, and
take such steps for the protection of the person and
property of natives as are consistent with the laws of
the land.

"Sub-section 3. In regard to natives not residing in
the Transvaal (a) he will report to the High Com-

missioner and the Transvaal Government any encroachments reported to him as having been made by
Transvaal residents upon the land of such natives,
and in case of disagreement between the Transvaal
Government and the British Resident as to whether
an encroachment has been made, the decision of the
Suzerain will be final ; (*b*) the British Resident will
be the medium of communication with native chiefs
outside the Transvaal, and, subject to the approval of
the High Commissioner, as representing the Suzerain,
he will control the conclusion of treaties with them ;
and (*c*) he will arbitrate upon every dispute between
Transvaal residents and natives outside the Transvaal
(as to acts committed beyond the boundaries of the
Transvaal) which may be referred to him by the parties
interested.

"*Sub-section 4. In regard to communications with
Foreign Powers, the Transvaal Government will corre-
spond with Her Majesty's Government through the
British Resident and the High Commissioner.*"

Another important reservation was the right to move
troops through the said State in time of war, but the
reservation considered at the time, and which events
subsequent thereto have proved most necessary, was the
right to control the external relations of the said State,
including not merely the conclusion of treaties, but the
conduct of its diplomatic intercourse with foreign
Powers, and all such intercourse was to be carried on
through Her Majesty's consular and diplomatic officers
abroad.

With regard to natives also, the functions to be

performed by the British Resident were proper and salutary, and were, in fact, entirely in accord with the views expressed by Mr. Kruger and his friends.

There are many other provisions in the Convention, relating to boundaries, native locations, settlement of debts, &c., but none of them materially affect the questions of to-day as between Her Majesty as suzerain and the Boer Oligarchy. (An exact copy will be found in the appendix.)

Article 32 only need be mentioned :

"This Convention will be ratified by a newly elected Volksraad within the period of three months after its execution, and in default of such ratification this Convention shall be null and void."

It was beyond a doubt understood that this new Volksraad should be elected by all the inhabitants who were entitled to vote, but this provision was not complied with, and thus the first infringement of the compact was winked at by Her Majesty's Ministers. The "Convention" was signed at Pretoria on August 3, 1881, by Hercules Robinson, President and High Commissioner; Evelyn Wood, Major-General; J. H. de Villiers.

Let us now recapitulate the rights conceded by Her Majesty to the inhabitants of the Transvaal, as set forth in the Convention of 1881.

1st. Self-government, with the franchise guaranteed to all inhabitants under laws then existing.

2nd. Full liberty to reside in the State, to possess houses, manufactories, warehouses, etc.

3rd. To carry on commerce, either in person or by agents, and to be subject to no taxation whatever other than might be imposed on Transvaal citizens.

And lastly, No law should be passed inconsistent with or repugnant to the provisions of this Convention.

Hence we see that any alteration in the laws then existing, extending the time or altering the conditions under which aliens might obtain Burgher Rights in the State, any laws which interfered with the free enjoyment of property, or the personal liberty of such alien, or any law fettering him in the exercise of his trade, commerce, or industry, or in the establishment of manufactories, is a direct violation of this Convention, and that all persons so aggrieved have a perfect right, morally, legally and equitably, to require from Her Majesty the fulfilment of her guarantee.

Whatever was demanded by the Commissioners, and acceded to bỹ the Boer representatives with whom they conferred, must be taken to be the definite conclusions of both sides, and whatever is expressed within the four corners of the Convention is to be taken as the spirit of the agreement, and the intentions of the parties thereto.

No evasion is possible. Each condition, reservation or limitation, set out in the articles of the Convention, was discussed at length by the Boer leaders before it was accepted, and, as we gather from the reports of the conferences, every argument which a subtle mind could bring to bear upon each question under debate, was

G

adduced by the able Hollander legal adviser of the Boers, Dr. Jorissen, as well as by the delegates themselves. A study of what took place at these interviews demonstrates the keen penetrative shrewdness of President Kruger, and his marvellous capacity for evading any issue either compromising to himself, or adverse to the object he has in view.

Nor must the magnificent services rendered by Sir Evelyn Wood, on our side, pass unnoticed. He proved himself to be more than a match for his wily adversaries. His knowledge of the facts, and his grasp of the situation, appear on every page, whilst every one who reads these documents must be struck with astonishment at the legal acumen and diplomatic ability displayed by this man, a soldier, not a statesman.

CHAPTER V

THE SURRENDER OF 1884

ORDINARILY, on the settlement of a dispute, after terms and conditions have been agreed to, reduced to writing and signed by duly accredited representatives of both opposing interests, the matter is looked upon as finished, and each side considers itself bound by the document so executed. Not so the Boers. If they fail to get their own way in a deal, they consider that they have been wronged, and must at once set to work to redress the imagined grievance, for the fact of having to submit to any restrictions, real or fancied, is in their eyes an aggravation of the injustice done them. Bearing this in mind, one can readily account for the conduct of Mr. Kruger and his co-signatories when they faced their Volksraad and produced the "Convention" for ratification.

Secretly, they had stirred up the members of that body, who were all like themselves disaffected, to protest against the terms and conditions which the Triumvirate had signed. This protest was lodged with the object of reopening the whole question when a favourable opportunity offered, and although the members of the Volksraad sanctioned the Convention, they did so with the understanding that every step would be taken to have its provisions speedily upset.

Their objections and alternatives were mainly as follows :

(1) Instead of the direction of foreign affairs by Her Majesty's Government, there should only be supervision thereof.

(2) There should be no interference with the future legislation of the country, either with regard to the white inhabitants, or to measures affecting the interest of native tribes.

(3) The Resident should simply be the representative of the Sovereign, but should possess no further authority.

(4) The Transvaal should receive compensation from Great Britain, for the territory east and west which had been taken, and that the debts of the country should only be paid by the burghers after those debts had been proved lawfully to exist.

Mr. Kruger came over again to this country with the object of advocating the reconstruction of the Convention on these lines. Whilst here, he and his able legal adviser who accompanied him, had ample opportunities afforded them, not only of studying from our Blue Books the policy which Mr. Gladstone's Cabinet had laid down to the Royal Commissioners in 1881, but also the trend of British affairs generally, the condition of Ireland, at that time, occupying the attention of the Government in such a manner as to exclude all minor considerations ; such for instance as the affairs of the Transvaal State. Although they had to depart from England without having effected any change in the Convention, they were well aware that, as long as the Liberal Government kept in office, there was every hope of eventual success in the direction at which they were aiming, viz., at all hazards and by every means to destroy or evade its provisions.

It must be borne in mind that these objects were continually kept in view by the Boer delegates, and no blame can possibly attach to them or to the other leaders of the movement, determined like themselves to get rid of every obligation imposed by the Convention. Their desire was to render the Transvaal territory free from control of Her Majesty as suzerain, and they naturally took advantage of the weakness and vacillation evinced by the Government of the day, to become emancipated from all surveillance.

These Commissioners, profiting by the knowledge gained in England, on their return to Pretoria proceeded to disseminate their views amongst the Boers, and agitated within and without the Volksraad to have those Articles of the Convention which were repugnant to their notions of freedom either recast or expunged. Now, from the manner in which the Boers were even then treating the Suzerain in the question of the franchise by flagrantly setting the Convention at defiance, they felt they could advance their pretensions with impunity, and, no matter what their action, that Mr. Gladstone's Ministers would never cause a shot to be fired against them to enforce Her Majesty's authority.

For, in open disregard of Article 3, a law was passed

in 1882 providing that, before a new comer could become naturalised and acquire full rights of citizenship, he must have resided in the country for a period of five years, must have been registered on the Field Cornet's list for that period, and pay a sum of £25. This law, opposed to the spirit and intent of the Convention of 1881, was actually in force in 1884, and was passed unquestioned by Her Majesty's Government when, in that year, the second Convention was signed in London.

It is not surprising, then, that in 1884, after all their experience of British indecision and apathy, the Boers should make another bold effort to cancel all, or as many as they could, of the terms, conditions, reservations, and limitations obnoxious to them, but which they had accepted scarcely two and a half years before. Once more President Kruger accompanied by two delegates, Mr. S. J. du Toit and Mr. N. J. Smit, visited England to try and accomplish the object for which he had incessantly striven, this time with a clever Hollander lawyer named Beelaerts van Blockland in his train, and without loss of time they approached Mr. Gladstone and Lord Derby, then Colonial Secretary. These Boer envoys knew their own minds, they determined to wipe out from the Convention of 1881 every article which militated against their independence as a Sovereign State, or which fettered in any way their right to frame laws affecting the interests of the Uitlander.

They did not quite succeed in carrying out the programme in its entirety, but a comparison of the two conventions shows that they went a long way towards it. Judging them from their own standpoint, the aims

of these Boer delegates were lofty and patriotic, and
because they took advantage of the weakness or
shiftlessness of their opponents, praise rather than
censure should be awarded them. But what can be
said in defence of those responsible Ministers of the
Crown, who had pledged Her Majesty in 1881 to
guarantee to all the inhabitants of the Transvaal
complete self-government, and the enjoyment of all
civil rights under her Suzerainty? The changes in
the second Convention are more than startling. In
the first place, *no allusion is even made to the Suzerainty
of the Queen, or to Her Majesty's guarantee set out at the
commencement of the Convention of* 1881 !

That the omission was made designedly there can be
no doubt, and indeed, to-day the Boers allege that
under the 1884 Convention no Suzerainty exists.
That, in fact, Her Majesty through her Ministers
contracted herself out of the exercise of all suzerain
authority, save only the shred of it expressed in
Article 4, whereby the South African Republic agreed
not to conclude any "treaty or engagement with any
State or nation other than the Orange Free State, nor
with any native tribe to the eastward or westward of
the Republic, until the same has been approved by Her
Majesty the Queen."

The fallacy of such a contention is apparent when
these two documents are compared, for be it clearly
understood that no alteration was made in the form of
guarantee of complete self-government, given by Her
Majesty in 1881, to all inhabitants of the Transvaal
State subject to her Suzerainty. Unlike the declaration
at the commencement of the 1881 Convention, there is

a preamble to the Convention of 1884, setting forth the reasons for the modification *of articles* embodied in its predecessor and, when we construe the legal and binding effect of this later agreement, that preamble must be taken in conjunction with Her Majesty's former declaration in 1881, as Suzerain, which was in no way abrogated or even mentioned in the Convention of 1884.

It will then be made clear to the most obtuse intellect that Her Majesty's rights as Suzerain remain intact, Her guarantee holds good, and the 1881 Convention in these respects is in full force *subject solely to the articles of the Convention of* 1884 *being substituted for those of* 1881.

A glance at the preamble alluded to above will demonstrate the accuracy of my deductions.

Whereas . . . that the Convention ratified by the Volksraad of the Transvaal State, "on the 25th October 1881, contains certain provisions which are inconvenient, and imposes burdens and obligations from which the said State is desirous to be relieved, and that the South-western boundaries of the said State should be amended, with a view to promote the peace and good order of the said State, and of the countries adjacent thereto; and, whereas, Her Majesty the Queen of Great Britain and Ireland, has been pleased to take the said representations into consideration : Now, therefore, Her Majesty has been pleased to direct, and it is hereby declared that the following *articles of a new Convention* . . . shall, when ratified by the Volksraad of the South African Republic, be *substituted for the articles* embodied in the Convention of 3rd August, 1881."

Not the articles alone, but the entire convention of 1881, was inconvenient to the Boers, and imposed burdens and obligations on the State, from which Paul Kruger, his burghers, and Hollander friends, naturally wished to be relieved; and, indeed, the most important article of all they had abrogated, as we have seen, during the interval, without the formality of consulting Her Majesty. This was by the law passed by the Volksraad in direct violation of the Convention of 1881, enlarging the time for an alien to become enfranchised from two to five years.

But, it must be confessed that these Boers succeeded in obtaining more relief than even they anticipated. Mr. Gladstone and his Ministers agreed to a change of name from the Transvaal State, insisted on in 1881, to that of the South African Republic, thus favouring the contention now put forward that the Transvaal must no longer be considered a vassal State, but an independent Sovereign Power.

The Boers desired to be relieved of the "burden and obligations" of having a British Resident to intervene in any question between them and natives, and they had also discovered that it might prove extremely "inconvenient" if the Suzerain should exercise her right to move troops through the Transvaal in time of war. But still more onerous was it that the Transvaal State could only conduct its diplomatic intercourse with Foreign Powers through British channels; therefore, those articles of the Convention of 1881, embracing these stipulations, were all calmly expunged from the Convention of 1884.

How Mr. Gladstone and his Cabinet came not only to countenance, but also to sanction, these Boer-cum-Hollander pretensions remains a mystery. We can only conclude that Her Majesty's Government were either so weak, or so deaf to all sacred obligations towards others, or so afraid that they lost their heads. Even at this day, with all the faults and failures of Mr. Gladstone's Irish policy before us, one is at a loss to imagine what influences were brought to bear on the Cabinet at that time sufficient to ensure the signal triumph of these Boer and Hollander envoys. Remember, no change of Ministry had taken place. The men who were eager to tear up the terms and conditions imposed by themselves in the Convention of 1881, held office in 1884 with one exception. Lord Kimberley was no longer Colonial Secretary, and Lord Derby reigned in his stead. So that those responsible advisers of the Crown could not allege that their policy on this question was contrary to that of another political party who had imposed the terms of the former Convention two and a half years before.

They possessed a full knowledge of all the facts as reported to them at the time, and since that period, by their own distinguished and trusted officials. They had their own despatches, based on those reports, before them to refer to. They had listened to and had rejected the arguments and allegations which the Boers advanced, and yet they deliberately set aside as valueless their former convictions, and departed from the rules which ordinarily guide English statesmen. In short, this group of politicians sacrificed the rights of every man who had ·unfortunately trusted to their compact, and surrendered to President Kruger and his advisers the most important conditions, limitations, or reservations, which two and a half years before they had promised, in the name of Her Majesty, that the Boers, and indeed, all the inhabitants of the Transvaal, would be compelled to observe.

To make my contention perfectly plain, I append, below, the declaration of 1881, in parallel columns with the preamble of the Convention of 1884, and also those articles of the earlier Convention side by side with what was substituted for them in 1884. By this means every one will be enabled to form his own opinion of the diplomatic victory gained over Her Majesty's "Little Englanders" by the Boer envoys and their distinguished Hollander adviser, who, it is said, drafted the Convention.

CONVENTION OF 1881.

Her Majesty's Commissioners for the Settlement of the Transvaal territory, duly appointed as such by a Commission passed under the Royal Sign Manual and Signet, bearing date the 5th of April 1881, do hereby undertake and guarantee on behalf of Her Majesty that, from and after the 8th day of August 1881, complete self-

1884.

Whereas the Government of the Transvaal State, through its Delegates, consisting of Stephanus Johannes Paulus Kruger, President of the said State, Stephanus Jacobus Du Toit, Superintendent of Education, and Nicholas Jacobus Smit, a member of the Volksraad, have represented that the Convention signed at Pre-government, subject to the suzerainty of Her Majesty, her heirs and successors, will be accorded to the inhabitants of the Transvaal territory, upon the following terms and conditions, and subject to the following reservations and limitations :—

toria on the 3rd day of August 1881, and ratified by the Volksraad of the said State on the 25th October 1881, contains certain provisions which are inconvenient, and imposes burdens and obligations from which the said State is desirous to be relieved, and that the southwestern boundaries fixed by the said Convention should be amended, with a view to promote the peace and good order of the said State, and of the countries adjacent thereto ; and whereas Her Majesty the Queen of the United Kingdom of Great Britain and Ireland has been pleased to take the said representations into consideration: Now, therefore, Her Majesty has been pleased to direct, and it is hereby declared, that the following articles of a new Convention, signed on behalf of Her Majesty by Her Majesty's High Commissioner in South Africa, the Right Honourable Sir Hercules George Robert Robinson, Knight Grand Cross of the Most Distinguished Order of Saint Michael and Saint George, Governor of the Colony of the Cape of Good Hope, and on behalf of the Transvaal State (which shall herein-after be called the South African Republic) by the above-named Delegates, Stephanus Johannes Paulus Kruger, Stephanus Jacobus Du Toit, and Nicholas Jacobus Smit, shall, when ratified by the Volksraad of the South African Republic, be substituted for the articles embodied in the Convention of 3rd August 1881; which latter, pending such ratification, shall continue in full force and effect.

ARTICLE II.—Her Majesty reserves to herself, her heirs and successors, (a) the right from time to time to appoint a British Resident in and for the said State, with such duties and functions as are

ARTICLE IV.—The South African Republic will conclude no treaty or engagement with any State or nation other than the Orange Free State, nor with any native tribe to the eastward or west-

herein-after defined; (*b*) the right to move troops through the said State in time of war, or in case of the apprehension of immediate war between the Suzerain Power and any Foreign State or Native Tribe in South Africa; and (*c*) the control of the external relations of the said State, including the conclusion of treaties and the conduct of diplomatic intercourse with Foreign Powers, such intercourse to be carried on through Her Majesty's diplomatic and consular officers abroad.

ARTICLE III.—Until altered by the Volksraad, or other competent authority, all laws, whether passed before or after the annexation of the Transvaal territory to Her Majesty's dominions, shall, except in so far as they are inconsistent with or repugnant to the provisions of this Convention, be and remain in force in the said State in so far as they shall be applicable ·thereto, provided that no future enactment especially affecting the interest of natives shall have any force or effect in the said State, without the consent of Her Majesty, her heirs and successors, first had and obtained and · signified to the Government

ward of the Republic, until the same has been approved by Her Majesty the Queen.

Such approval shall be considered to have been granted if Her Majesty's Government shall not, within six months after receiving a copy of such treaty (which shall be delivered to them immediately upon its completion), have notified that the conclusion of such treaty is in conflict with the interests of Great Britain or of any of Her Majesty's possessions in South Africa.

[No corresponding Article appears.]

of the said State through the British Resident, provided further that in no case will the repeal or amendment of any laws enacted since the annexation have a retrospective effect, so as to invalidate any acts done or liabilities incurred by virtue of such laws.

ARTICLE XII.—All persons holding property in the said State on the 8th day of August 1881 will continue after the said date to enjoy the rights of property which they have enjoyed since the annexation. No person who has remained loyal to Her Majesty during the recent hostilities shall suffer any molestation by reason of his loyalty, or be liable to any criminal prosecution or civil action for any part taken in connection with such hostilities, and all such persons will have full liberty to reside in the country, with enjoyment of all civil rights, and protection for their persons and property.

ARTICLE VII.—All persons who held property in the Transvaal on the 8th day of August 1881, and still hold the same, will continue to enjoy the rights of property which they have enjoyed since the 12th April 1877. No person who has remained loyal to Her Majesty during the late hostilities shall suffer any molestation by reason of his loyalty; or be liable to any criminal prosecution or civil action for any part taken in connection with such hostilities; and all such persons will have full liberty to reside in the country, with enjoyment of all civil rights, and protection for their persons and property.

ARTICLE XIII. — Natives will be allowed to ' acquire land, but the grant or transfer of such land will, in every case, be made to and registered in the name of the Native

ARTICLE XIX.—The Government of the South African Republic will engage faithfully to fulfil the assurances given, in accordance with the laws of the South African Republic,

Location Commission, hereinafter mentioned, in trust for such natives.

ARTICLE XIV.—Natives will be allowed to move as freely within the country as may be consistent with the requirements of public order, and to leave it for the purpose of seeking employment elsewhere or for other lawful purposes, subject always to the pass laws of the said State, as amended by the Legislature of the Province, or as may hereafter be enacted under the provisions of the Third Article of this Convention.

ARTICLE XVI.—The provisions of the Fourth Article of the Sand River Convention are hereby re-affirmed, and no slavery or apprenticeship partaking of slavery will be tolerated by the Government of the said State.

ARTICLE XVIII.—The following will be the duties and functions of the British Resident :—

Sub-section 1. He will perform duties and functions analogous to those discharged by a Chargé d'Affaires and Consul-General.

Sub-section 2. In regard to

to the Natives at the Pretoria Pitso by the Royal Commission in the presence of the Triumvirate and with their entire assent, (1) as to the freedom of the natives to buy or otherwise acquire land under certain conditions, (2) as to the appointment of a commission to mark out native locations, (3) as to the access of the natives to the courts of law, and (4) as to their being allowed to move freely within the country, or to leave it for any legal purpose, under a pass system.

ARTICLE VIII.—The South African Republic renews the declaration made in the Sand River Convention, and in the Convention of Pretoria, that no slavery or apprenticeship partaking of slavery will be tolerated by the Government of the said Republic.

ARTICLE III.—If a British officer is appointed to reside at Pretoria or elsewhere within the South African Republic to discharge functions analogous to those of a Consular officer he will receive the protection and assistance of the Republic.

natives within the Transvaal State he will (*a*) report to the High Commissioner, as representative of the Suzerain, as to the working and observance of the provisions of this Convention ; (*b*) report to the Transvaal authorities any cases of ill-treatment of natives or attempts to incite natives to rebellion that may come to his knowledge ; (*c*) use his influence with the natives in favour of law and order; and (*d*) generally perform such other duties as are by this Convention entrusted to him, and take such steps for the protection of the person and property of natives as are consistent with the laws of the land.

Sub-section 3. In regard to natives not residing in the Transvaal (*a*) he will report to the High Commissioner and the Transvaal Government any encroachments reported to him as having been made by Transvaal residents upon the land of such natives, and in case of disagreement between the Transvaal Government and the British Resident as to whether an encroachment has been made, the decision of the Suzerain will be final; (*b*) the British Resident will be the medium of communication with native chiefs outside the Transvaal, and, subject to the approval of the High Commissioner, as representing the Suzerain, he will control the conclusion of treaties with them; and (c) he will arbitrate upon every dispute between Transvaal residents and natives outside the Transvaal (as to acts committed beyond the boundaries of the Transvaal) which may be referred to him by the parties interested.

Sub-section 4. In regard to communications with foreign powers, the Transvaal Government will correspond with Her Majesty's Government through the British Resident and the High Commissioner.

ARTICLE XXIV.—The independence of the Swazis within the boundary line of Swaziland, as indicated in the First Article of this Convention, will be fully recognised.

ARTICLE XII.—The independence of the Swazis, within the boundary line of Swaziland, as indicated in the first Article of this Convention, will be fully recognised.

ARTICLE XXV.—No other or higher duties will be imposed ou the importation into the Transvaal State of any article the produce or manufacture of the dominions and possessions of Her Majesty, from whatever place arriving, than are or may be payable on the like article the produce or manufacture of any other

ARTICLE XIII.—Except in pursuance of any treaty or engagement made as provided in Article IV. of this Convention, no other or higher duties shall be imposed on the importation into the South African Republic of any article coming from any part of Her Majesty's dominions than are or may be imposed on the like

country, nor will any prohibition be maintained or imposed on the importation of any article the produce or manufacture of the dominions and possessions of Her Majesty, which shall not equally extend to the importation of the like articles being the produce or manufacture of any other country.

article coming from any other place or country; nor will any prohibition be maintained or imposed on the importation into the South African Republic of any article coming from any part of Her Majesty's dominions which shall not equally extend to the like article coming from any other place or country. And in like manner the same treatment shall be given to any article coming to Great Britain from the South African Republic as to the like article coming from any other place or country.

These provisions do not preclude the consideration of special arrangements as to import duties and commercial relations between the South African Republic and any of Her Majesty's colonies or possessions.

ARTICLE XXVI.—All persons, other than natives, conforming themselves to the laws of the Transvaal State (a) will have full liberty with their families to enter, travel, or reside in any part of the Transvaal State ; (b) they will be entitled to hire or possess houses, manufactures, warehouses, shops, and premises ; (c) they may carry on their commerce either in person

ARTICLE XIV.—All persons, other than natives, conforming themselves to the laws of the South African Republic (a) will have full liberty, with their families, to enter, travel. or reside in any part of the South African Republic ; (b) they will be entitled to hire or possess houses, manufactories, warehouses, shops, and premises ; (c) they may carry on their commerce either in per-

or by any agents whom they may think fit to employ; (*d*) they will not be subject, in respect of their person or property, or in respect of their commerce or industry, to any taxes, whether general or local, other than those which are or may be imposed upon Transvaal citizens.

·ARTICLE XXVII.—All inhabitants of the Transvaal shall have free access to the Courts of Justice for the protection and defence of their rights.

son or by any agents whom they may think fit to employ; (*d*) they will not be subject, in respect of their persons or property, or in respect of their commerce or industry, to any taxes, whether general or local, other than those which are or may be imposed upon citizens of the said Republic.

[No corresponding Article appears.]

With what little respect the Boers regard any conditions embodied in a solemn compact, we gather further from their conduct at the time these negotiations were in progress for the substitution of Articles in the Convention of 1884, for those assented to in 1881. For example, no boundary line was ever considered sacred, and Transvaal Boers at that very period had trekked over the border into territory under British protection, established themselves therein, and Her Majesty's Government were compelled to send a strong force under Sir Charles Warren to drive them out, the cost of that expedition to the taxpayers of this country being upwards of one million sterling.

Their triumph over Mr. Gladstone in 1884 was for some time of no real value to the Boers, for, left to themselves, they sank back into the same financial slough which had engulphed them before annexation became a necessity in 1877. Taxes were not paid and revenue could not be raised. In addition, miners who, during the annexation, had been successfully working goldfields in different parts of the Transvaal, notably in the Barberton, Lydenburg, and Zoutpansberg districts, became distrustful of the Government, and either discontinued developments or opened up no new ground.

To such a pitch of depression did the Boers arrive, that it was seriously mooted to ask Her Majesty to again come to their rescue and administer the country. However, about the year 1886, a sudden change came about, without their seeking, which relieved them from the throes of incipient bankruptcy. This was the discovery of gold in payable quantities in Witwatersrand, and the rush of men consequent on these finds put a very different complexion on the Boers' financial position. Emigrants poured into the district, capital was attracted, and suddenly a city, Johannesburg, sprang up far exceeding in population and importance Pretoria itself. Then came the opportunity of Boer and Hollander, and they were not slow to avail themselves of the chances Dame Fortune threw in their way. Instead of fostering this great industry by passing liberal measures for the common good, they regarded it only as a means whereby the lucky few in power could extort plunder. The Boers in the swim, with the aid of their Hollander subordinates, amassed wealth beyond the dreams of avarice. They looked on the Uitlander, whose money filled their pockets, as a mere instrument sent by the Almighty for their special benefit. Corruption became rampant, and all consideration for Conventions or obligations was thrown to the winds the instant

it stood in the way of Boer and Hollander aggrandise-
ment.

Concessions and monopolies in defiance of the Convention were granted in shoals to those who were
willing to share profits with the inner ring. At first,
whilst the new comers were rapidly making and losing
fortunes through wild-cat gambling concerns, little
attention was paid to Boer cupidity or impositions, but
as soon as matters had sobered down, and this seething
community learnt that the extraction of gold even in
Witwatersrand must be conducted on business principles, a sudden change set in.

When it became apparent that honest returns in the
shape of dividends must be paid to those shareholders
in other countries who had invested money in these
mining enterprises, every one naturally looked to the
Government not to impose restrictions which would kill
the industry. But, here again, Hollander astuteness
and Boer cunning were under-estimated. The former
went on making hay while the sun shone, the latter
through greed, ignorance and race hatred, looked on
the Uitlander as his natural prey. In making these
statements, however, it is necessary to use discrimina-
tion, for my remarks apply mainly to the little circle in
office at Pretoria. The Boer outside this coterie has
not sufficient intelligence to enable him to understand
how he is being hoodwinked. A sop is thrown to one
by the payment of £300 per annum as a member of the
Second Volksraad, to another by an appointment to a
salaried post created especially for him in his district.
All each one knows is that the Government at Pretoria
pays him, and in consequence he does what is required.

Still the Boer on the Veldt is a factor with which we shall have to reckon. One continuous cry is echoed from Pretoria all throughout the Transvaal. "Your independence is threatened by the Uitlander, be prepared to fight as your fathers did in defence of this sacred cause." By every vile means does the servile Hollander press keep alive race hatred, and one day, not far distant, if great care be not exercised, Mr. Kruger, his Oligarchs and Hollanders, will discover that they have raised a Frankenstein which will devour them. Long ago every shadow of pretence of respecting the Convention vanished. The Boer-cum-Hollander Ring has excluded every outsider from a share in the administration, or a voice on questions of taxation and expenditure, although nine-tenths of the revenue comes out of Uitlanders' pockets. No alien can acquire burgher rights, neither is he free to establish any business in face of a monopoly granted to others. His children must receive their instruction in the public schools in Dutch! The press has been muzzled! ·

The right of public meeting is denied! He can be expelled from the country at the sweet will of the Executive and he has no remedy before the tribunals of Justice. Until the repeal of the immigration law recently announced, he could not move freely in and out of the country without a pass, thus being on the same footing as a Kaffir. And, lastly, the authority of the Supreme Court has been practically subordinated to the whims or rascality of about thirty men, who comprise the Executive and the so-called Conservative majority in the Volksraad. And yet we are told that no steps should be taken by the Suzerain to protect the inhabitants of the Transvaal, to whom she guaranteed complete self-government and the enjoyment of all civil rights!

Still less has any inquiry been made into the treatment Kaffirs have received at the hands of the Boers. All Her Majesty's duties towards the unfortunate natives were conveniently ignored in 1884, when the functions of the British Resident were deliberately excluded from the new Convention. This dereliction has been most serious, for every Uitlander as well as Kaffir in the South African Republic is labouring under the effects of Mr. Gladstone's cowardly surrender of supervision over the truculent Boer in his relations to the black man, and at any moment retribution may be exacted. To appreciate this we must examine into the injuries already inflicted on some native tribes, and must remember that others may be exposed any day to similar treatment by these uncivilised Boers.

CHAPTER VI

BOER TREATMENT OF THE KAFFIR

Persons who picture the ordinary Boer as a model of piety, rough and rude, but honest and deeply religious, form a very highly coloured estimate of his character. On the contrary, at heart and in habits he is the same narrow-minded bigot, with the identical notions of his right to enslave the Kaffir, as was his father the Voortrekker. The old Testament is his standard, and he rarely wanders beyond its first four Books.

Of the doctrines of forgiveness, charity and mercy, as exemplified in Christ's teaching, he is absolutely ignorant, and, had Trooper Halkett been a Boer, our Lord's words would have made no more impression on him than on a rock.

Boer proneness to enslave the black man was manifested by the Sand River Convention, wherein a special clause was inserted to prevent this practice. All to no avail, and again, in 1881, it was deemed imperative, in view of the infractions of the Sand River Convention relating to slavery, again to insert the declaration in the Convention of that date. Once more it was embodied in the Convention of 1884, Article 8 of which runs thus : "The South African Republic renews the declaration made in the Sand River Convention and in the Convention of Pretoria, that no slavery will be tolerated by the Government of the said Republic."

In defiance of this Article, I maintain that in many districts, under the form of apprenticeship, Kaffir children and youths have been over and over again enslaved by the Boers. Let us proceed by steps. In the Blue Book, C 1776, p. 9, presented to both Houses of Parliament in April 1877, there appears a graphic extract from the *Cape Argus*, dated December 9, 1876, descriptive of atrocities committed on Kaffir tribes by the Boers, both in 1868 and at that date. This account corresponds so nearly with what I witnessed with my own eyes in 1895, that I append a portion of that extract, and later I shall proceed to narrate what has come under my own observation.

"In the year 1868, a public meeting was held at Potchefstroom, in the Transvaal, to consider the war then going on with natives in the district of Zoutpansberg. Some statements were made at that meeting which have a singular relation to what is now going on in the district of Lydenburg. In 1868 innocent blood was shed by commandoes, and Government officers were guilty of treachery. Such things are done again in 1876. Lest we should be charged with exaggeration, we shall let our witnesses speak for themselves. First; as to the atrocities mentioned at the meeting in 1868. One of the speakers was the Rev. Mr. Ludorf, and, according to a report of the proceedings at the meeting, he said, 'That on a particular occasion a number of native children, who were too young to be removed, had been collected in a heap, covered with long grass and burnt alive ; other atrocities had also been committed, but these were too horrible to relate.' Called upon to produce proof of this horrible story, the reverend gentleman named his authority in a solemn declaration to the State Attorney. At the same meeting, Mr. J. G. Steyn, who had been Landdrost of Potchefstroom, said : 'There now was innocent blood on our hands which had not yet been avenged, and the curse of God rested on the land in consequence.' Mr. Rosalt remarked that 'It was a singular circumstance that in the different Colonial Kaffir wars, as also in the Basuto wars, one did not hear of destitute children being found by the commandoes, and asked how it was that every petty commando that took the field in this Republic invariably found numbers of destitute children. He gave it as his opinion that the present system of apprenticeship was an essential cause of our frequent hostilities with the natives.' Mr. Jan Talyard said, ' Children were forcibly taken from their mothers, and were then called destitute, and apprenticed.' Mr. Daniel van Vooren was heard to say, ' If they had to clear the country, and could not have the children they found, he would shoot them.' So much for the statements made regarding the sacrifice of innocent blood. As to treachery, Mr. Field-cornet Furstenburg stated that when he was at Zoutpansberg with his burghers the Chief Katse-Kats was told to come down from the mountains ; that he sent one of his subordinates as a proof of amity; *that whilst a delay of five days was guaranteed by Commandant-General Paul Kruger, who was then in command, orders were given at the same time to attack the natives at break of day, which was accordingly done, but which resulted in total 'failure.'* So much for what was done in 1868.

"Let us now see what is done in 1876. We would gladly give the names of our authorities here also, but that it might, among other things, place their lives in danger. We hear one gentleman has been threatened because he is supposed to correspond with some newspaper. Another tells us that it is necessary to preserve the closest secrecy at present, and that it is only under the protection of the British Government that the whole truth could be divulged. It is reported in the *Natal Colonist*, that letters supposed to be for newspapers in the British Colonies are in some cases tampered with in passing through the Transvaal. Under these circumstances it is necessary, apart altogether from the ordinary rule of keeping the name of a correspondent secret, that the correspondents in the Transvaal who speak the truth should be guarded from the dangers apparently attached to their position. We, therefore, are compelled to withhold their names, even if we otherwise were disposed to give them, but we pledge ourselves as to the high position and reputation of our informants. Not many weeks ago a friendly kraal was attacked, and women, children, and cattle captured. An order from the President compelled the farmers to release their victims, but threats were uttered that in a short time were put into effect. Kaffir allies were sent to destroy the women and children, and about sixteen were put to death. There is a field-cornet called Abel Erasmus, who recently visited a kraal of friendly natives, when he off-saddled and partook of the hospitality of the people, the chief giving him a goat to slaughter.   Thirteen natives were commandeered from this kraal and accompanied an expedition commanded by Abel Erasmus.   On the third day the men were told to go home by Erasmus, as he intended returning, and after they were deprived of the ammunition in their possession they went back to their kraal. Not suspecting any danger, they were sleeping in fancied security, when about dawn the next morning Erasmus attacked their kraal, killed three old men who were sitting round a fire, wounded a man and a woman, and took six women and eighteen children prisoners. He also captured a number of cattle, and threatened if more were not given to kill the chief and all his people. It is this same Erasmus who, according to the telegram we publish to-day, has attacked another friendly chief and shed more innocent blood.   On this point, therefore, and it will be noted that we only give examples of what takes place, 1876 is on a par with 1868."

Mr. Abel Erasmus was not dismissed after these outrages, and as time passed his zeal met with its reward in his promotion to the important post of Commissioner over the Lydenburg district.   I am indebted to leading articles in the *Zoutpansberg Review*, published no longer ago than the 5th and 13th of April of the present year, for the exposure of this man's latest atrocities.   But before I quote from that journal, it is incumbent on me to draw attention to the manner in which the Convention of 1884 has been wilfully and contemptuously broken, where the rights guaranteed to Kaffirs are concerned.

No person who has not lived among natives can form an adequate idea of the injustice done to them, or how often the rights granted them by the Convention have been disregarded. These wrongs have often been inflicted through the stupidity, wilful neglect, or cupidity of minor Government officials, but the Government itself is to blame for making such injustice possible, and by framing laws in direct opposition to the spirit of the agreement of 1884. Now, Article XIX. of the Convention of that date stipulates as clearly as words can express that

"The Government of the South African Republic will engage faithfully to fulfil the assurances given, in accordance with the laws of the South African Republic, to the natives at the Pretoria Pitso by the Royal Commission in the presence of the Triumvirate and with their entire assent,

"1. As to the freedom of the natives to buy or otherwise acquire land under certain conditions.

"2. As to the appointment of a commission to mark out native locations.

"3. As to the access of the natives to the courts of law, and

"4. As to their being allowed to move freely within the country, or to leave it for any legal purpose, under a pass system."

The Pretoria Pitso referred to took place at the time of the retrocession in 1881, when Sir Owen Lanyon, speaking on behalf of the British Government, addressed the native chiefs and headmen who had assembled from all quarters.   He spoke as follows :

> *" Paramount Chiefs, Chiefs, and Natives of the Transvaal !*

"You are called together by us, the representatives of the Queen of England, to be informed what Her Majesty's Government has resolved to do with reference to the future ruling of this country.

"You are aware that, somewhat more than four years ago, the Transvaal was annexed to the possessions of the British Empire.   This was done because it was then believed that the majority of those who had a voice in the ruling of the country desired such annexation in preference to the Government of those who were then in power.   Subsequent events have shown that this belief was wrong, and Her Majesty's Government, with that feeling for justice proper in a great and mighty nation, commanded that the country should be handed back to its former rulers, under certain conditions, which have been drawn up by us, and agreed to by the representatives of the burghers.   I have now much pleasure in presenting to you these representatives, Messrs. Kruger, Pretorius, and Joubert.

"In the conditions to which they, as I have said, agree, your interests have not been overlooked.   All existing laws will be enforced, and no future laws, which more particularly affect your interests, will be put in force until the Queen has approved of them.   I desire that you will to-day distinctly understand that although an alteration will take place in the form of government, your rights as well as your duties will not undergo any alteration.

"It will be allowed you to buy land, or to acquire it it in one way or another, but the title will be registered to you in the name of three gentlemen who will constitute a Native Location Commission. The Commission will survey, point out, and beacon off native locations, which the large native tribes may occupy in peace. With the surveying of such locations, existing rights will be strictly enforced; and the Transvaal Government of the one part, and the native tribes of the other part, will have to recognise and respect the boundaries as laid down. In the same manner the different tribes will have to respect each other's locations, and where this is not done the aggrieved tribe will lay their complaint before the Government of the country.

"At the restoration of the country to the burghers, the Queen reserved the right to appoint a British Resident here, and it will be one of the special duties of this official to see that the provisions of the Convention are carried out in your favour. I am pleased of the opportunity this day to introduce to you the person who will fill this important position, and to recommend you all to his care. I must, however, caution you against the idea that he will be the ruler of the country. The Government will be the ruler, subject to Her Majesty's Suzerain rights, but the Resident will report the same, whenever he has convinced himself that the natives have been maltreated, or whenever any attempt has been made to induce them to rebellion. At the same time he will always be prepared to assist you with his advice, and I am convinced that such advice will be conducive to law and order.

"The different Law Courts will always be open to hear your grievances, and to restore your rights, and I trust that you will never have any reason to complain to the Resident that the portals of justice had been closed to you. Reflect that you are looked on as a law-abiding people, and that it will be allowed to nobody to take the law into his own hands. You will do well to close your ears against mischief-makers, whether English, Africander, or Native, who might attempt to lead you from the right path.

"When you require protection against your enemies you must wend your way to the Government of the country to which you pay your taxes, whose duty it is to grant you protection. As I have remarked before, we have entered into an agreement with the representatives of the burghers regarding the ruling of the country, and if you desire more explicit information regarding your rights under this agreement, the Resident will always be prepared and willing to supply you with the desired information. With two points I will, however, acquaint you now. Provision is made that no slavery will exist, or anything approaching it. This proviso existed in a former Convention, and the Transvaal representatives have agreed and consented that it will again be established. So every one may now know what the law on this subject is. But you must bear in mind that working for an honest wage does not constitute slavery, and that you will never be lifted from your present state, until experience has taught you that honest labour is no disgrace whether performed by men or women.

"The other point is that it will be allowed you to travel about the country, or leave the same, with the object of seeking work elsewhere, or for other lawful purposes. It will however be necessary to retain the present Pass Law, with the object of carrying out and preserving good order.

"What the Transvaal now requires is enterprise, unity, and peace. When the inhabitants, whether white or coloured, will each carry out the work for which they are fit; when they will unite to forward the interest of the country, and forget for ever differences and disputes, and carry out the principles of peace and union, then this country will very surely have a clear and brilliant future to look to.

"The Queen desires the welfare of you all, and you can be assured that although this country is on the point of being restored to its former rulers, your interests will never be forgotten or neglected by Her Majesty's Government, or by Her Representatives in South Africa.

"Now you will all go back in peace to your kraals, and acquaint all your friends with the words I have spoken to you this day."

Practically, the control over natives, and their destinies, is exercised by one man who has recently attracted attention by the part he played in the Jameson raid. This personage is none other than Commandant Cronje, who, as Superintendent of Natives, appears to be endowed with unlimited power.

Instead of acting as a Court of Appeal in native cases from the decisions of the Native Commissioners he frequently, during the course of his flying visits through the country, dispenses summary justice without reference to the Courts. It is a matter of notoriety that the present holder of the office has given cause for much dissatisfaction among the natives by the scant attention he pays to their complaints, and by the roughness of his treatment towards them. The other day at Lydenburg he personally inflicted a heavy fine under most unjust circumstances. The case referred to is that of the Paramount Chieftainess of Sikukuni's tribe, Toerometsjani, who has been worried for a considerable period on most frivolous pretexts. She was fined £147 10s. by Commandant Cronje for not paying taxes, although the money was offered to, and refused by, him ; and this was only one of a long series of persecutions and outrages which this unfortunate woman has undergone.

It becomes necessary to examine into some of the methods which the Boers have adopted to express their contempt for the article of the Convention, referring to the Pitso at Pretoria in 1881.

By an Executive resolution of January 21, 1894, rules were published for dealing with native cases before the Native Commissioners, and it was thereby stipulated that no native could employ an agent to appear on his behalf before first obtaining the sanction of the Government. The necessary and farcical course to be followed by the native in such a case is to make application to the Native Commissioner, who in turn passes it on to the Superintendent of Natives, who refers the matter to the Executive Council, who, more often than not, refuses the application after due consideration.

It is therefore an absurdity to tell the native that the Law Courts are always open to him, as the contrary is the reality, and hundreds of cases have fallen to the ground because the assistance of an agent has been refused, or unobtainable. The native is not generally a good pleader of his own cause after the fashion of the white man, and the services of an agent are absolutely necessary in important cases in order that he be not cheated out of his rights.

The Special Court consisting of the Native Commissioner, the Superintendent of Natives, and the Executive is a miserable failure, in which the natives have no confidence, and the High Court is practically closed to them.

Again, by Law 24 of 1895, an extra personal tax of £2 was imposed on each native, independent of the ordinary hut-tax in existence at that time. This measure was also not submitted for Her Majesty's approval.

Law No. 21 of 1895, known as the Squatters' Law, provides that no person may have more than five natives on his farm, so that a native is not at liberty to live where he would be likely to obtain work, for no matter how willing the farmer may be to engage him, he cannot go against the law by having six boys on his farm. There is not much use in pointing out to the native the dignity of labour when he is handicapped in this fashion from obtaining it.

According to the Convention (Art. 19, sub-sec. 3) the Government is bound to respect the regulations detailed at the Pretoria Pitso as regards the locations of natives, but this part of the agreement is more honoured in the breach than in the observance, more especially in the manner of surveying, placing beacons, and the custody of the title-deeds. These latter important documents are supposed to be in the hands of the Superintendent of Natives, and might as well have never existed, for all the benefit they are to the native.

It is hardly necessary to add that this state of affairs is distinctly opposed to Her Majesty's pledges to the native chiefs in the presence of the Triumvirate, Messrs. Kruger, Joubert and Pretorius.

The whole wide question of the treatment of the Native tribes in the Transvaal demands immediate investigation and settlement. That duty devolves upon Her Majesty in her capacity as Suzerain, and is in accordance with her acknowledged obligations. In the early part of this book it has been shown how the Boers in 1876 and 1877 could not conquer Sikukuni, and that in 1879 Sir Garnet Wolseley was compelled to subdue him. Therefore the fortunes of the paramount chieftainess of Sikukuni's tribe will, I venture to think, be interesting to British folk. I append the story of her recent sufferings taken from the *Zoutpansberg Review* of April 13, 1897 :

" Some five years ago a tribal row occurred between the followers of Geluk and Sikukuni, on account of which the chieftainess or Queen-Regent, Toeromets-jani and her chief indunas were sent to Pretoria with

her son, the juvenile paramount chief, Sikukuni, who
was about to be educated at the Government expense
with a view to the better undertaking of his duties
when he came of age. Gobalala, the next in rank, was
a trusted friend of the chieftainess and acted as her
deputy in the location, but was in bad odour with the
Native Commissioner, the notorious Abel Erasmus;
while another chief, Golaan, the son of Geluk, aspired
to secure the paramount chieftainship for himself, and,
Toerometsjaṇi maintains, that he was aided and abetted
by the Native Commissioner. Abel Erasmus acted the
rôle of sovereign lord of all the tribe, and was assisted
in all his plans and forays by Golaan, who supported
him through everything, with an eye to his own future
advantage; the majority of the tribe, however, would
not acknowledge Golaan as their head. The result of
this disturbance was that a number of Sikukuni's
people, who were under Gobalala, were sent to gaol at
Pretoria, without the slightest attempt at a judicial
investigation being made.

"In January 1896, some natives walked into
Pietersburg, a distance of about 100 miles from their
location in the Lydenburg district, to ask for assistance,
as Gobalala, who was still acting for the absent chieftainess, and his people were being attacked by Abel
Erasmus and his armed burghers, supplemented by a
number of natives belonging to the pretender, Golaan.

"The armed whites, assisted by Golaan's party, then
ravaged the country, seizing Gobalala's cattle and
goats, and shooting down a number of natives who
attempted to flee for their lives. The procedure
followed was the sending out of a mounted party under

the orders of Erasmus and the command of Schoeman, to disarm any of Gobalala's people they might fall in with. These unfortunates never made any organised resistance, as they had only defended themselves against the attacks of Golaan's people, but many gross acts of cruelty were perpetrated during this disarming process. A few instances may be mentioned to illustrate the cold-blooded barbarity of these proceedings. A native named Hendrik Morothani, who was a catechist, or following some similar calling, belonged to Gobalala's tribe, and at the time of the disturbances was living at Pretoria, where his chieftainess was also residing, but in an unlucky moment he resolved to visit his location. Before Gobalala came into Erasmus's camp, a party of Golaan's men intercepted Morothani's waggon and shot him and his leader dead, without the slightest provocation, and took his waggon and oxen into Erasmus's camp. When Gobalala arrived on the scene, Erasmus told him of the shooting, and intimated that he was to take it as a warning. The waggon oxen were distributed among Abel Erasmus's party.

"Again, a party of burghers, assisted as usual by Golaan's men (armed always with Gobalala's surrendered arms), came up to a native kraal, in which lived a headman named Dingoe, and a few others, which they found deserted by all except the women. They forced the women to disclose the hiding-place of the men, a hole in the side of a hill a short distance from the kraal, and here Dingoe and four or five others were concealed. The party opened fire into this hole ; the natives returned the fire, but could not be dislodged, although one was killed and others wounded. A fire

was then kindled at the mouth of the hole, and the
women were compelled to fetch pots of fat to add fury
to the flames.   As even this did not succeed, the party
rode away.   When the natives emerged from their
oven they were in a terrible state, their hair, even to
the eyelashes, their clothing, and their wounds being
all severely burnt.

"Abel Erasmus and his party then began dividing the
spoil gathered in the several forays, each man receiving
so many head of cattle, and Gobalala and his men were
taken to Lydenburg as prisoners.

"However, before these disturbances came to an end
in this highly dramatic manner, Erasmus summoned
another chief, one N'Kwaan, who had taken no part in
the fighting, to bring in his men and assist this despotic
Native Commissioner.   N'Kwaan refused to place
himself in the hands of Erasmus on the grounds that
he did not live in the location and belonged to neither
party, and that he was afraid, as he had previously
lodged complaints in Pietersburg against Erasmus for
taking more tax-money from him than he was entitled
to ; that Erasmus had not given proper receipts for the
tax-money he received ; and that during the Magoeba
war Erasmus had commanded him to pay an extra £2
a head as a war-tax, and therefore he knew that if he
went he would be made a prisoner, and some pretext
found for seizing his cattle.   It is necessary to explain
that if this unauthorised war-tax was not paid on the
first day of demand, the amount was doubled on the
second day, trebled on the third, and so on ; and
that with regard to the receipts for ordinary taxes,
these were made out in such a purposely muddled

manner that the same person was often compelled to pay taxes over and over again. Such receipts as 'Received from Klaas, and 19 others' were the general rule, bearing only a stamp mark, and no signature.

"The doubting N'Kwaan went to Pietersburg to seek advice under these circumstances, when it was reported that Abel Erasmus was about to attack him. He caused the whole matter to be reported to General Joubert, stating that he had had nothing whatever to do with the disturbances, and was ready to defend himself in a court of law against any charges that might be brought against him. This letter had a good effect. Erasmus was checkmated, and N'Kwaan was safe—so far.

"All these combined circumstances impressed General Joubert, who immediately set out for Lydenburg, where he found the luckless Gobalala and his men in gaol. He sent these to Pretoria to await further investigation, and about a week later the chieftainess Toerometsjani, and her son the youthful paramount chief, Sikukuni, with their headman, were allowed to leave Pretoria for their location. During the time the General was in Lydenburg he appointed a Commission, of which Abel Erasmus was a member, to make a division of the location lands for the sake of peace and order, giving Gobalala's people the one side and those of Golaän the other. When installing the chieftainess, the General said that peace must be maintained, and that he would give them time to get in their crops, after which they must settle on either the one side or the other. The dividing Commission gave the best grounds to Golaan and his people, and much dissatisfaction was caused among the other natives who were allotted the less fertile and dried-up portions. Gobalala was released at Pretoria by General Joubert, and a small balance of his cattle that had been recovered was ordered to be restored to the chieftainess.

"So matters were apparently settled, but were in reality in a worse state than before, for the chieftainess had no grain, as all the crops had been destroyed by the filibusters, and rinderpest, locusts, and drought had completed the havoc. She therefore caused a letter to be written to the new Superintendent of Natives, Commandant Cronje, which had to pass in its official course through the hands of the Native Commissioner, Abel Erasmus, begging for assistance, and asking that the special tax of £2 a head, and the ordinary taxes for that year, be not enforced owing to her poverty-stricken condition. No reply was vouchsafed to this.

"Later on, the famine pressed so heavily on her people that she asked for Government assistance in mealies, stating that her people were dying from starvation. No reply was received.

"She also wrote to Commandant Cronje asking that Abel Erasmus be removed from the post of Native Commissioner, as he was her enemy, and had killed some of her people, and that his treatment of the natives was one of persecution. This letter, like the others, was sent through Erasmus, and was not answered.

"When his Honour the President, accompanied by Commandant Cronje, paid his visit to Pietersburg in October last, a party of Sikukuni's people came over from Lydenburg to state their grievances and ask help, and Commandant Cronje said he would go over to Lydenburg and see them there.

"Erasmus now gave notice to the natives that he was coming to collect taxes, and his clerk, van der Wall, appeared in the vicinity of the location with a white man from Johannesburg in attendance. The chieftainess explained that as all her people were starving they could not pay, as they had no money. Van der Wall replied that the gentleman from Johannesburg who was present, would advance the money to pay the taxes if she gave him a sufficient number of men to work at the Rand mines. This she did not care to do, as she was afraid if she took this money that she would place herself in the power of the dreaded Erasmus. She, however, sent messengers to Pietersburg to explain the case, and endeavour to raise the money there.

"The sum of £1200 was brought from Pietersburg by some well-known residents of that town, and the chieftainess sent to van der Wall, who was in the location, to come over to her head kraal, and receive his taxes. But he refused absolutely to go to the kraal to take the money. Shortly after this he sent word that he had referred the matter to Pretoria. The bearers of the money waited for eight days, and then returned to Pietersburg. The offer to pay was afterwards renewed, and again refused.

"In the early part of December, Commandant Cronje, Superintendent of Natives, fulfilled his promise by arriving at the location at Lydenburg and fulfilled it with a vengeance. He was accompanied by Abel Erasmus, Native Commissioner, David Schoeman, Sub-

Native Commissioner, Winter, an ex-missionary and a factotum of Erasmus, and several other white people. The Superintendent sent for the chieftainess and all her headmen and also for the chief N'Kwaan.   He then said that complaints had been laid against her by Abel Erasmus, amongst other things (1) that she had ordered her tribe not to pay money to the tax-collector unless it was paid in her presence. (This she had done in compliance with the terms of the law.) Another complaint (2) against her was that when the rinderpest broke out in her location she did not give proper notice of the fact. (3) That the natives living outside her location made complaints to her of which she took notice. (This referred to some of Golaan's people who through not understanding the new location arrangement continued to live in their old quarters.) (4) That some of her petty chiefs had also not reported an outbreak of rinderpest. (5) That she had objected to Abel Erasmus as Native Commissioner, and had asked that another be appointed. (6) That she made use of agents, instead of stating her troubles to Abel Erasmus, her Native Commissioner. (This charge was *the* sore point of the case.) (7) That men living outside her location were also ordered by her not to pay taxes unless in her presence. (This charge is explained by the fact that when N'Kwaan found himself pressed by Erasmus, who threatened to prosecute him under the Squatters' Law, he with another petty chief, came into the location and settled under the chieftainess, but there was no one to point out the position of the beacons, and Erasmus contended that some of them had settled down just outside the boundary.)

"Toerometsjani denied the truth of these charges, except those about asking for the removal of Erasmus, and that the taxes should be paid in a regular manner in her presence, according to law. The unexpected result was that, without calling witnesses, or investigating the matter in the slightest degree—and indeed the investigation of these trumped-up charges would have been a sickly farce—the chieftainess was fined £147 10s. and all her headmen, to the number of about twenty, *were ordered to receive twenty-five lashes each.* After Commandant Cronje departed the flogging was inflicted. The backs of the innocent victims were severely lacerated, Abel Erasmus flogging one man himself, and Schoeman several others. The humorous Schoeman required each man to say 'dank u baas' after his flogging, and those who refused received an extra lash. The Commandant violated the law of the land, and his subordinates the justice of the Commandant.

"The chief N'Kwaan, with his crippled interpreter, Jonathan, were also brought up to be flogged. Abel Erasmus took advantage of this opportunity, and told N'Kwaan that some time ago he was fined £100 by Schoeman as some of his girls had spread rinderpest, and that he was also fined £10 for not assisting Erasmus in the trouble with Gobalala, and he now ordered him to pay these fines at once. This was the first word the astounded N'Kwaan had heard of the fines, and he begged for time to pay, but Erasmus said he was only too glad to get hold of him, and both the chief and his interpreter were marched off to gaol, with their hands so tightly tied that their arms became swollen. A Pietersburg agent sent the amount of the fines £110, for the release of the prisoners, but the omnipotent Erasmus would not accept it, saying N'Kwaan must stay in gaol for two years, but Jonathan was released. This was a nice *finale* to an appeal for help, natives being punished on groundless complaints, without evidence, law, or justice.

"The above is but one sample of how the natives are treated in one district of the country, and every district has its own tale of persecution to relate. What a mockery are the words of Sir Owen Lanyon to the natives at the time of the retrocession, 'The Queen desires the welfare of you all, and you can be assured that although this country is on the point of being restored to its former owners, your interests will never be forgotten or neglected by Her Majesty's Government, or by her representatives in South Africa.' Only sixteen years ago since that promise was made, to be unheeded and forgotten already!"

As it happens, my acquaintance with Boer warfare against Kaffir tribes was formed in that same district of Zoutpansberg, over which in 1868, President Kruger then Commandant-General, held command. Zoutpansberg possesses a fertile soil and varied climate, to an extent unknown in any other portion of the Republic. It stretches northwards to the Chartered Company's border, and eastward to Portuguese territory. It is almost the last home of Kaffirs living together in a tribal state.

Now, the coach road from Pietersburg, the capital of the province, to Leydsdorp in the "Low Country," a distance of ninety miles, passes through some of the finest scenery to be met with in the Transvaal. On the route, mountains have to be climbed and descended, deep gorges to be negotiated, and in the rainy season rapid rivers have to be forded.   Yet ordinarily, setting aside the dangers incidental to your driver piloting eight mules and the coach at a hand gallop round a bluff, where, if he gets off the track, there are only a few feet between you and eternity, or if on rushing a river he gets stuck, and his passengers and mules run the risk of being drowned, the journey is delightful to a man in good health.

On leaving Haenetsburg the road stretches for a considerable distance through treeless undulating Veldt, but if one is travelling after the first spring rains, the grass will be found a vivid green, save where it is carpeted by innumerable flowers, whilst in every dell may be descried large tree ferns spreading their graceful fronds, one of the features of that region.   On reaching the summit, and before descending, the coach is halted to allow heavy steel slippers to be adjusted to the hind wheels, for the way for some miles thence is perilously steep.

But whilst this short stoppage is made we can look around, and no man who has once been there can ever forget the magnificent panorama presented to him.   On his left, extending for miles along the mountain slopes, lie the Woodbush forests, looking in the magnificent distance like an array of English parks, whilst below them again is a glorious, broken, wooded landscape, with here and there the bright gleam of a river, and stretching away to the horizon.   On the right, rise the bold escarped peaks of the Drakensburg range, whilst in front can be perceived a narrow, coloured thread, winding round and over a green lower range of hills, indicating the road the coach must traverse ere it reaches its destination.

On the top of one of these hills stood the kraal of Mashuti, a minor Kaffir chief. You approached his town through a picturesque gorge, climbing as you proceeded; the road on each side shaded by large trees with here and there a wild banana spreading its broad leaves, giving a semi-tropical appearance to the scene. Embowered as it was, a traveller could form no idea of the extent of this kraal from the rapid glimpse obtainable of the roofs of the huts, but it was always a cheerful feature of the journey to see the small nude black children, who, having no fear of the Englishman, would show themselves and cheer the occupants of the vehicle as it passed swiftly along.

Mashuti's people were peaceful and industrious; they cultivated mealies over a large area which he and his folk had occupied for generations, and they possessed a considerable number of cattle, sheep, and goats. They menaced no one, and never interfered with the few Boer farmers in their vicinity. But in 1894, they had to reckon with Boer cupidity and greed. Longing eyes had been cast on their herds and lands by unscrupulous Field-cornets and others; the usual game began, unjust demands for hut taxes which were resented; then followed lying representations to Pretoria, only too eagerly listened to, as to the dangerous character of the tribe. A commando was sent against them. Naturally they attempted to defend their hearths and homes, but in the end were almost wiped out, their lands confiscated and their cattle, under the name of loot, apportioned amongst their murderers.

The attack was made just before the rainy season commenced and the survivors of this poor tribe were driven to seek what shelter they could with other Kaffirs, or to die of starvation and exposure, as numbers did, on the Veldt. When last I passed Mashuti's kraal, though some time had elapsed since the slaughter, I could still see vestiges of calcined clay huts, and innumerable bullet marks on the stones.

Successful in this raid on Mashute, the same gang adopted similar measures towards neighbouring tribes in the Woodbush, whose chiefs were Magoeba and Madjadjie. Here, owing to the nature of the country, and the thick bush or forests into which the Kaffirs retired, their task was not so easy. But a large commando was raised, and so-called forts were built at great expense a long distance from the Kaffir stronghold. No one ever dreamed for an instant that these forts were necessary, or that the few wretched Kaffirs being hunted, at most 800 men, armed only with assegais and a few obsolete muskets, would ever attack them, but the pretence served its purpose to obtain for each man on commando £15 per month and a share of loot. I shall never forget as long as I live the appearance of these cowardly loafers, who would have taken a lease in perpetuity of their position, when on two occasions whilst their supposed operations were in progress I passed by these so-called forts.

Ultimately, however, the scandal became too grave even for the Boer Government, and a strong contingent of Swazis, thanks to Great Britain, who for years past had been hereditary enemies of the Woodbush tribes was organised and sent against them. Within a fortnight they accomplished what for months the valiant Boers had failed to do. No check was imposed on the indiscriminate slaughter which ensued, Magoeba was slain and decapitated, and the poor wretches who escaped wounded, maimed, or dying, scattered themselves over the Low Country.

It was publicly stated by the Zoutpansberg press at the time, that numbers of children were taken by the Boers, under the guise of making them apprentices, and though I have no personal knowledge on that head, still I have sufficient reliable hearsay evidence to convince me of its accuracy. However, I myself caused shelter and food to be given to more than one batch of these miserable creatures, amongst them being women and children, some of them wounded. A pathetic incident connected with these massacres remains to be told. Not once during the fighting did the Kaffirs cut the telegraph wires or stop the coach, though they could have done either at any time. Their reason was that they regarded coach and telegraph as being " Englishman's property " and not as belonging to the Boers.

Had the terms imposed by the Convention of 1881 been adhered to, and the functions of the British Resident at Pretoria been maintained, these murders and robberies would never have occurred, but as we know, Mr. Gladstone, in 1884, agreed with President Kruger that to safeguard the lives, persons, and property of natives, was not obligatory on Her Majesty.

But then Kaffirs are not Christian Armenians, Bulgarians, or Levantine scum, whose practical Christianity bears as much affinity to the teachings of Christ as does that of a Chinaman, so that this powerful reason may, perchance, have influenced Mr. Gladstone and his colleagues. At any rate, the righteous restraint put on the Boers, mainly by Sir Evelyn Wood, who knew his men, was removed, and the Article of the Convention establishing the duties of a British Resident towards natives obliterated, as one of the "certain provisions which are inconvenient and imposes burdens and obligations from which the said State desires to be relieved."

This, too, in the face of the clause inserted in the Sand River Convention, their own conditions imposed in 1881, and again reiterated in the Convention of 1884, which they were about to sign. And still some men are to be found who squirm at the phrase "unctuous rectitude"11

CHAPTER VII

THE HOLLANDER

PRESIDENT BURGERS had paid a visit to Europe prior to 1877, with the joint object of obtaining money, and of arousing different nationalities to take an interest in the Transvaal State. He naturally spent some time in Holland, the land whence his ancestors originally sprang, and whose language was the official tongue of himself and his fellow countrymen. Stimulated by his descriptions, and by hopes held out of future wealth to be gained in the Transvaal, several Hollanders emigrated to South Africa, and some were inducted into official posts at Pretoria. That they soon took an active part in Boer politics we have learnt from Sir T. Shepstone's narrative. Nor did they cease their zealous propaganda against British rule, nor fail to aid President Kruger in his secret agitation after his return from England in 1879, for though they took no part in fighting us, Hollanders were ever present in council to direct and suggest the tactics to be pursued, in order to enable the Boers to accomplish their purpose. With all his shrewdness and natural ability, Paul Kruger is incapable of presenting his views in a manner intelligible to educated men without assistance, and thus, perhaps unconsciously, he has daily learnt to rely more and more on skilled Hollander advice, until at last both he and his Boer Executive have become absolute puppets in the hands of this grasping group.

The progress in this direction has been slow but certain. Let us trace it.

When hostilities had ceased and the convention was duly signed, it became necessary for these peasant Boers, many of whom could not write their own names, to give practical effect to the self-government which Her Majesty had guaranteed to the inhabitants of the Transvaal State. Obviously their mode of life and ignorance of all departmental details, as well as of the administration of justice, unfitted them for the performance of their part of the compact. Recent events had caused them to mistrust, with few exceptions, the cultured Afrikanders of the Cape Colony, Natal, and the Orange Free State, many of whom by training and experience were admirably qualified to fill either the highest executive or other posts. It was further out of question that an Englishman could be admitted to share their confidence or their councils.

One Hollander lawyer resident in the country, Dr. Jorrisen, as we have seen, had taken a prominent part with President Kruger, firstly in opposing the annexation, and secondly in the negotiations with Sir Evelyn Wood, and he had naturally not only greatly influenced the Triumvirate but had aided them by his legal knowledge.

It is not strange, therefore, that they looked to Holland to supply them with men capable of assuming those functions which in every State appertain to

the management or control of governmental requirements.

As a result, Hollanders were gradually introduced
into the country, and soon monopolised the public
service.   More especially was such the case after the
visit of President Kruger to Europe at the beginning of
1884; for on that visit he met with, and engaged the
services of an astute and clever Hollander, Dr. Leyds,
whose personality next to that of the President himself
has loomed large in the subsequent history of the
Transvaal State.   From the advent of Dr. Leyds to
Pretoria, we can trace what may be aptly termed the
Hollander invasion, and the carrying out of the tacit
but well understood Hollander policy, viz. : *that the
form of government of the South African Republic must
be an oligarchy composed of ignorant Boers who must in
turn be ruled by Hollanders, to the material advantage of
the latter.*

Ever soft and suave and outwardly deferential to the
Boers, the Hollander official never loses an opportunity
of adroitly suggesting to their narrow minds, the
injuries which he alleges have been inflicted on them
by the British.   By means of flattering phrases, deftly
turned, appealing to their patriotic vanity or courage,
he worms himself into their good graces.   This he is
enabled to do the more readily as it forms no part of the
Hollander's policy to thrust himself forward as the
chief of a State Department, such as Railways or
Mines.   The figure-head must be an uneducated Boer,
whose want of knowledge affords the staff every chance
to act as they please, and to enrich themselves.

It will be found also in nine cases out of ten where

retrogressive or vindictive measures have been passed by the Volksraad in defiance of the Convention, that these have been secretly inspired by one or more of the Hollander clique. And so cleverly was this managed, that the dull-witted Boers have been brought to believe the idea sprang from their own slow brains. Again, when any friction occurs, occasioned now and then by petty legislative oppression, but generally by some flagrant act of injustice aimed at Uitlanders' interests, the Hollander is always there to insinuate that here is another proof of British duplicity and treason.

When President Kruger returned home in 1884, after his celebrated victory over Mr. Gladstone and Lord Derby, his country was in a state of absolute bankruptcy, and there was then little scope for the display of the talent for intrigue which Dr. Leyds has since manifested. In fact, so hopeless was the financial position considered, that more than once it was seriously debated by many leading Boers to ask Her Majesty to resume control of the Government.

However, with the discovery of gold on the Witwatersrand and the consequent impetus given to the development of that portion of the Transvaal, mainly by Englishmen and Afrikanders from Kimberley and Barberton, a mighty change took place. Hollanders saw their opportunity and they took advantage of it to the full. Mining laws had to be altered to suit the rapidly growing advance of immigrants and capitalists, and a number of new posts had necessarily to be created, and additions to be made to the higher and lower magistracy.

It was soon decided by the capitalists interested in

the goldfields, that more rapid and cheaper means of communication than that which a coach or ox waggon supplied must be provided, so with the enterprise characteristic of the energetic spirits in Cape Colony, headed by Mr. Rhodes, a railway was pushed through the Orange Free State to the Vaal River. These men, moreover, found the money, some £700,000, when the Boers had no credit, for its extension to Johannesburg and Pretoria. Here was a splendid chance for wary Hollanders to create for themselves a monopoly of all railway construction and working in the South African Republic. Their labours resulted in the concessions granted to the Netherlands Railway with its enormous privileges, high tariffs, impudent disregard of the rights of the great community whose servant it ought to be, and generally the corrupt influence which it has exercised, and still continues through its officials.

Once a monopoly had been granted, the door was naturally opened for the creation of others, and on the principle that you may as well be hanged for a sheep as a lamb, there was no stint in the number of concessions, arranged chiefly by the agency of complacent Hollanders. Neither has there been any concealment of the breaches repeatedly made of the Convention, though these have led to untold injustice and to the loss and suffering of the community. Take, for example, the dynamite concession.

No sane person could imagine that in a land where scientific mining has attained to a pitch of greater perfection than in any other country, the sole right to manufacture explosives, the most important article necessary for the extraction of ore and protection of human life, is enjoyed by one ring of monopolists. And yet such is the case. No factory can be erected for the fabrication of explosives except by Mr. Lippert, a German, and those interested with him in his concession. Not a single ingredient used in their cartridges is manufactured in the Republic, all are imported separately from Europe, and are mixed at the Company's works.

For a long time the article supplied by these monopolists was so inferior and uncertain in its action that many lives were lost consequent on its use. Personally I shall never forget the horrid appearance which the bodies of dead and mangled Kaffirs presented when hauled up the shaft of a mine to the surface after an explosion, the result of one of Messrs. Lippert and Company's defective cartridges.

But it is as a drag on the wheels of progress that the Hollander excels, and it is only right that we should consider his attitude towards the important question of education. For a long time a fight has been going on to compel children of different nationalities to receive instruction in public schools, through the sole medium of the Dutch language. Great indignation has been aroused by this stupid attempt to stifle knowledge, and especially among the English population, who enormously outnumber all others, and who know that any Englishman can travel from the Vaal to the Limpopo without once being called on as a necessity to speak Dutch. Somehow it seems to be accepted as gospel that these educational restrictions have been imposed by the Boers themselves out of a misguided spirit of patriotism, and a determination to make the

Dutch language paramount.   There is no more reason
for this belief than is there to suppose that all plead-
ings, evidence and procedure, in the courts of justice
are conducted in Dutch purely to expedite business.

No ; here the work of the wily Hollanders is only
too plain.   At this hour the Chief of the Education
Department, the most bitter opponent of liberal instruction and sternest upholder of the system, is a
Hollander.   Nor is the motive for their conduct far to
seek.   These worthies, who have temporarily left the
dykes of Holland and have become the political
advisers of a few obstinate farmers at present dignified
with the title of a government, know only too well that
if they wish to return to their native land with a good
store of guelders they must retard as long as possible
their inevitable expulsion.   Over the present generation
of uneducated Boers they have succeeded in obtaining
sway, and it is a subtle point in the game to keep the
rising generation also as ignorant as possible.

In the large towns such as Johannesburg and
Pretoria this is somewhat difficult, but we must not
forget that more than three-fourths of the Burgher
population is scattered over the Veldt.

Railways.

In few directions has the Hollander displayed to a
greater extent his rooted aversion to all progress than
in the construction of railways by others.

Working ever in the interests of the Netherlands
Company, this ring of Dutch officials have set their
wits to work to wreck or impede every railway enter-

prise in which they have no part, although in each instance had not the Netherlands Company declined to avail itself of its privilege to construct such roads on its own account the concession would not have been sanctioned.

Apart from the Netherlands Railway concessions two others have been granted, one to a Belgian syndicate, who afterwards formed a company to construct a line from Komati Poort, the station within the Transvaal on the Portuguese frontier to Leydsdorp, thus opening up the rich gold and mineral districts of the Murchison Range, Klein Letaba, Silati, Woodbush and Haenetsburg. These regions are also very fertile, and contain a large Kaffir population.

The circumstances under which this concession was obtained were such that to-day no legislator is anxious to refer to them, because officials and members of the Raad were bribed in the most unblushing manner ; in short, never did the Volksraad sanction a more flagrant piece of jobbery. This line should have been finished long ago, but all work has been abandoned on it for upwards of two years, and the portion already constructed will have to be again almost entirely rebuilt. Meanwhile, interest is being paid at the rate of 4 per cent. on the bonded debt of the road, or say £80,000 per annum, a sum almost equal to the entire revenue of the country previous to 1877, and this interest is at present forthcoming out of the funds furnished by the debenture holders themselves. Some time ago a quarrel arose between the Government and the Company, and Railway Commissioner Smit was despatched to Belgium to settle the difficulty. This functionary, who is bound body and soul to the Hollander faction, commenced legal proceedings against the concessionaires in the Belgian Courts, and these may be expected to be concluded about the Greek Kalends. No one for a moment believes in the sincerity of the litigation, it is regarded as a red herring dragged across the trail, so as to distract attention from the shortcomings of certain highly placed personages at Pretoria. Numbers of capitalists, prospectors and others, relying on the promise that the line would be made at once, spent large sums in exploration and in sinking shafts on these Low Country goldfields. Thousands of claims were pegged out, and from licences on the Murchison range alone the Government for the last four years has been receiving an average of £14,000 per annum.

Now, alas! many poor fellows who have clung with desperation to properties in which they have such faith have been driven to abandon them and the district as well. Were the line constructed, goods could reach the Range at a cheaper rate than to any other goldfield in the Transvaal, the distance from Delagoa Bay being about 250 miles. At present, every article, from a crowbar to a tin of condensed milk, has to be brought by way of Johannesburg or Pretoria, at a cost in carriage *from thence of at least £20 per ton.*

But this is not all. Owing to the rinderpest, no transport could be obtained for a long time, and even now only with the greatest difficulty. An almost unprecedented drought last year caused the Kaffirs' cattle to die of starvation, and ruined their mealie gardens, whilst myriads of locusts ate up any crops that could be saved by irrigation. For months the poorer Boers and the entire Kaffir population have been starving, attempting to sustain life on roots, locusts, and the carcases of their dead animals. Hundreds of men, women, and children, have died from sheer hunger, although they possessed money and could have purchased food had it been there. Their lives lie at the door of each knavish Hollander and corrupt Boer at Pretoria who, to serve his own ends, or to conceal his guilt, has impeded the construction of the Silati line! Had the railway been made, or partially finished, say through the Tsetse fly country, two or three cargoes of mealies could have been sent from the United States or Argentina through Delagoa Bay, and these lives would have been spared.

Neither must it be supposed that the authorities at Pretoria have been ignorant of the situation, or of public feeling in the Low Country respecting this railway. Three years ago, and several times since, public meetings were held at Leydsdorp, attended by burghers, claim holders, and tradesfolk, and petitions clearly setting forth their grievances, were sent to the Executive Government and the Volksraad. I myself and Mr. McQueen were elected at one of the meetings as delegates to the Government at Pretoria to represent the views of these burghers.

Promises were lavishly made us by President Kruger and the Executive, that the works would be commenced shortly, and as a sort of sop, a Hollander engineer, Mr. Mooyen, who was an employé of the Netherlands Company, and well known as the cleverest railway obstructionist in Africa, was sent down to study the best route for the future line.   This was about a year ago, but up to now nothing further has been attempted. In the meantime, the Boers and Kaffirs may starve, the patient, long-suffering prospector be ruined, the capitalist fleeced, and the foreign shareholders in every company whose properties are located in these districts sacrificed.

The other railway is a line from Pretoria to Pieters-burg, and will be eventually the great Transvaal Trunk line to the north.   It will pass through a part of Waterburg and Zoutpansberg, and will open up not only large proclaimed goldfields, but also the most extensive grain lands of the Transvaal.   For strategic purposes it is invaluable, as the only Kaffir tribes within the borders of the State now to be feared, are located to the north of Pietersburg, within forty miles or so of the proposed terminus.   Here again, rinder-pest, drought, locusts, and consequent famine, have caused frightful mortality amid the poorer Boers and Kaffirs, and brought to the verge of financial ruin many hitherto opulent farmers.

It will not be gainsaid that in any community calling itself civilised, every effort would have been made, on humanitarian grounds alone, to push on rapidly the construction of such a line during the favourable season of the year.   But no such sentiments influence the Hollander faction at Pretoria, and their friend Railway Commissioner Smit.

Recently, President Kruger made a journey over the ground to be traversed by this road, and at every stopping-place his burghers clamorously urged on him the imperative necessity for its construction.   He saw with his own eyes the fearful condition of the country and inhabitants, and in reply to numerous deputations, both at Pietersburg and Nylstroom, he promised that the line should be pushed on forthwith. But in these cases the President proposes, and Commissioner Smit, aided by his technical engineer, Mr. Mooyen, disposes ! For even whilst President Kruger was at Pietersburg he was informed by Mr. Wright, the contractor, who is supported by all the burghers in the two provinces mentioned, that he (Mr. Wright) had just received a notification from Commissioner Smit warning him that he proceeded at his own peril with the work on any section other than the first, until Mr. Mooyen had given his approval. And this, after all the surveys had been made and the plans deposited !

President Kruger told Mr. Wright to go on with the construction and he would protect him. But behold, a few weeks later, Mr. Wright was again informed by Commissioner Smit that he was doing the work at his own risk, and consequently the plucky Englishman had perforce to discharge 800 men and suspend operations. Zoutpansberg and Waterberg burghers, however, are now factors in the Transvaal ; they immediately rallied round the persecuted contractor, and demanded the resumption of work with such insistence at Pretoria that Railway Commissioner Smit and his Hollander wire-pullers felt it prudent to modify their arrogant pretensions, lest worse might follow.

The sole object of this unprincipled obstruction is to freeze out an English contractor, and preclude an enterprising English company from efficiently managing a railway within the South African Republic. Nevertheless, there is a formidable section of the more intelligent Boers who are becoming alive to these transparent devices. Grim, stern experience has taught them that a means of transport other than by ox or mule waggon must be found. They see that railways increase the value of their farms, and that their produce can be quickly conveyed to markets where there is an unlimited demand for everything they can grow. They are becoming galled by the Hollander and many resent his tutelage. As an example I append the speech of Mr. Jan de Beer on this railway obstruction in the First Volksraad on February 3rd last.

" Mr. Mooyen, Technical Inspector, £950.

" Mr. Jan de Beer wished to have this item erased altogether, for the person who filled the situation at present seemed to do his utmost to prevent the building of the Zoutpansberg Railway. The people of Waterberg and Zoutpansberg suffered under the obstruction of the Technical Engineer. It was terrible to see people in the North dying of hunger, while the building of the railway was prevented by the arbitrary conduct of the Technical Engineer. This was not to be suffered any longer. He would request the member of the Executive (Mr. Kock) who was present, to take notice of what he said, for he was tired of writing to the Executive. He'did not blame the Railway Commissioner as much as the Technical Engineer, who without any justifiable cause was crushing the people in the famine-stricken North under his heel. It was a shame that the Government should not be able to compel this Hollander, who was an impossible man, to be reasonable. If the speaker could take him in his fist and hurl him back to Holland he would do so, and would be rendering his district a great service. He had with his own eyes seen old people creeping about the district looking for food. Because the contractor for the line was not a Hollander, he was obstructed in every possible way by Mr. Mooyen. How was it that railways were formerly expeditiously constructed without a technical engineer? The item must be absolutely erased. Two years had passed now, and not a yard of the line had been constructed. He felt for the suffering people in Waterberg and in Zoutpansberg keenly, and would pray honorary members of the Raad to hearken to him, and meet their dire wants by speedy railway construction. He intended handing in a motion, *re* the matter.

"Mr. Tosen remarked that the item, irrespective of the person who filled the position, was on the Order. The question was if the situation was desirable. He certainly thought it was.

"Mr. Jan de Meyer said that he could fully agree with the facts brought forward by the member for Waterberg. He also blamed the technical engineer that poor people had to eat leaves, &c., in the north in order to sustain life. That the line had not yet been started, was due to arbitrary obstruction on the part of the technical engineer."

Stranger still, a large number of Boers from Waterberg, Rustenberg and Zoutpansberg, have trekked into Rhodesia, where they are settling on farms, preferring the just rule of the Chartered Company to the vagaries of the men at Pretoria.   To President Kruger, and even to Dr. Leyds, this exodus is far from satisfactory. Burghers can now be ill spared, much less when of their own free will they are moving into the country of the man whom his Honour stupidly regards as the Boer's mortal enemy.

Now the Boer, despite his sluggish ignorant nature, has deep down in his heart one great passion which quicker brains than his can readily rouse.   This sentiment is best expressed by one word—*Independence.* In reality he is only harking back, through his training and traditions, to those first motives and aspirations which prompted his fathers to trek into the wilderness. Independence, as he understands the phrase, is his aim and goal.   Only manifest to him that some obstacle is being placed in the way of his reaching this cherished object, and he is ready and willing to fight his aggressor to the death.   The cute Hollanders readily grasped this sentimental note in the Boer's character, and they have played on it for all it is worth.   Slowly but surely they have made themselves necessary to these rude peasants, until to-day they control the entire direction of affairs, internal and external.

We cannot blink the situation, for at this hour Hollander influence is paramount in the South African Republic.   They are the Uitlanders' deadliest enemy and, far beyond the Boers, with two or three notable exceptions, they are responsible for the later violations of the Conventions.   There can be no peaceful concord between Boer and Uitlander in the Transvaal until the Hollander power and influence are shattered.   It is they who have built up the present despotic rule, fostered an illiterate oligarchy, intrigued with a foreign State, and indoctrinated the ignorant peasant on the Veldt with the belief that his independence is imperilled. Should war break out, these Hollanders would not be met with in the field. On the contrary, the slow-witted Boer would be found raking their chestnuts out of the fire. Every breach of the Conventions has been either suggested or supported by this self-interested group. Every repressive or retrograding measure passed by the Volksraad has been drafted and insidiously carried by them. In fact, the Uitlander inhabitants of the Transvaal are to-day indebted mainly to this Hollander ring for the iniquitous gigantic monopolies, restrictions on education, shameful pass laws, muzzling of the Press, denial of the franchise, obstacles to railway construction, tampering with justice, and every other outrage on decency, impeding a human being from the enjoyment of his civil rights.

CHAPTER VIII

THE SITUATION TO-DAY

THE question will be asked, and rightly so, by every one who has read up to this point—what remedy do you suggest in face of these present difficulties? My answer is simple and direct. Let justice be done. Uphold the Suzerainty imposed, and the guarantee given in the name of Her Majesty in 1881, and demand from the Boer Government that the Articles substituted in 1884 for those of the former Convention be maintained and fulfilled. Perform that duty, late in the day though it is, towards the inhabitants of the Transvaal which the Conventions and their provisions involve. Deeds we demand now, not words!

If our so-called statesmen would only appreciate how tired the world is growing of torrents of words, and how for the past sixteen years Boers and Hollanders have discounted these periodical outbreaks of British politicians, and have played their own game of bluff with impunity, then there might be some hope. Sir Alfred Milner's arrival should be hailed with feelings of profound gratitude, not only because a strong tactful man is required at the helm of Cape Colony to-day, but also because a movement is being made at last by the Imperial Government.

True, the relief comes from an unexpected quarter, yet it is none the less valuable, since Her Majesty's Secretary of State for the Colonies, Mr. Chamberlain, was in 1881 and 1884 a member of Mr. Gladstone's Cabinet when the humiliating peace was made, and the subsequent surrender to the Boers took place. He, of all men of the present Government, possesses the knowledge of what was intended to be granted as a measure of justice to the inhabitants of the Transvaal by those Conventions.

Neither can it with fairness be imputed to Mr. Chamberlain that he has changed front in the matter. Assuming that he acquiesced in the policy of the Cabinet of 1881, and that he was a consenting party to the substitution of the Articles of 1884, assuredly the scope and intent of each Convention must be patent to his mind. Every person endowed with common sense will understand that, in demanding from the Boer Government the due observance of these Conventions, Her Majesty's Ministers are to-day simply complying with a sacred duty undertaken by the Crown towards the inhabitants of the Transvaal State. There can be nothing aggressive or improper in this attitude, and the Boers, if honestly disposed, have no grounds for resisting such a reasonable request. On the other hand, if this corrupt Oligarchy is determined to brave the Suzerain and ridicule the Conventions as it has done hitherto, then the only argument applicable is that of armed force, and the rule of the Boer will be for ever swept aside in the South African Republic.

Prejudice, tyranny, greed, and insult can be tolerated no longer by free men in a free land, despite the petty spite of Little Englanders, like Sir William Vernon Harcourt. This prominent politician was also a member of Mr. Gladstone's Cabinet in 1881 and 1884, and he has recently, contrary to his wishes, done this country a great service by rousing the national spirit on Imperial questions which involve the preservation of our honour and duties to our kinsfolk in South Africa.

For his political reputation, it would be more seemly did this descendant of the Plantagenets observe a severe reticence on matters associated with the abandonment of the colonists after Majuba, as these anti-patriotic outbursts, for purely party purposes, only increase the contempt with which Englishmen regard his vapourings. Instead of trying to hamper the Government and belittle England before the world, he could, as an ex-law-officer of the Crown, do his country and his Sovereign yeoman service were he to point out that only under the Convention of 1881 does Her Majesty derive her right of Suzerainty over the South African Republic, and that the word Suzerain is not even mentioned in the Convention of 1884—especially as now the situation has become grave indeed.

Within the past few months, the Boer has armed himself to the teeth at Uitlanders' expense. He has imported from Germany many mercenaries instructed in the handling of heavy and light artillery, and skilled in the latest military tactics. He has built forts in well-chosen positions, and all this time, with the full knowledge of what has been going on, our sapient rulers have folded their arms, blandly smiled, or indulged in that now famous platitude: "We are, and ever will be, the paramount power in South Africa!" A lovely sonorous phrase which can always be relied on to bring down the British gallery! But men in South Africa have suffered too long from placing confidence in this kind of froth, and they now require *deeds!* They have not forgotten the asseverations of the present Commander-in-Chief, then Sir Garnet Wolseley, in 1880, that the Transvaal would be "under British rule as long as the sun shone, and until rivers ran backward!" Nor yet, that within a year of that distinguished prophecy, Mr. Gladstone, aided by some of those who are so valiant on paper to-day, broke his own and all other pledges, caused us to scuttle out of the country, and handed over all the residents therein white and black to the tender mercies of a few illiterate Boers and astute Hollanders.

The blame for this present state of affairs in the South African Republic lies mainly at the door of Her Majesty's Government, for the Boer has been taught by us to despise our strength and our diplomacy. He began to do this from the fatal moment when, after Majuba, Mr. Gladstone and his Ministers, in spite of Sir Evelyn Wood's advice, ordered that officer to make a humiliating peace. Step by step, the Boer's contempt for us has increased in proportion to our surrender of every principle insisted on in the first Convention. Our want of firmness and backbone has been his opportunity, and, as we know, prompted by his wily Hollander allies, he has ultimately set at defiance every important Article which was retained in that disgraceful document, the Convention of 1884. Ay, and even before that Convention was signed we have seen how deliberately the spirit and intention of the former one of 1881 was violated in the matter of the franchise. Had Her Majesty's Ministers insisted on the due observance of those Articles, we should not have now to deplore a Jameson raid, and the world at large would have been spared the unsavoury spectacle of our national dirty linen being publicly washed by Little Englanders in the tub of a Parliamentary Committee. This supineness, weakness, or indifference on the part of Her Majesty's Government—call it by whatever name you may—has had far-reaching consequences in other directions, for thereby a few unscrupulous capitalists have persuaded the Boer Government to go further than even they otherwise would have done.

These individuals openly winked at many breaches of the Conventions so long as they were profiting themselves. Only too well have Transvaal officials learnt that the terms of the articles were to be subservient to the personal interests of those who were ready and willing to pay a bribe for that privilege, and thus it has come about that huge monopolies, which are gigantic frauds on the rest of the community, have been granted to those who would agree to share the plunder with one or more persons in authority. The situation has also fostered a group of crawling plutocrats, who now profess great friendship for the Transvaal Government, and who appear happily oblivious of the fact that every shady step by which each has climbed the ladder of wealth is known to Mr. Kruger and his Hollander satellites. Were it not repugnant to one's sense of decency, it would be amusing to watch how these sycophants debase themselves for greed before the ignorant peasant legislators at Pretoria. As soon as one of the tribe rushes off to the seat of government, with proffers of service and protestations of zeal, another one speeds after him with the intent, in gambling parlance, of " going one better."

The next day, cablegrams descriptive of what took place at alleged interviews appear in our newspapers, generally through the medium of the Anglo-Boer subsidised journal in this country, only to be corrected, or their accuracy officially denied, a day or two later.

But outside these small groups of corrupting Uitlanders and grasping Boers and Hollanders are the masses of the foreign population resident in the country, suffering from outrageous restrictions on their persons and property. And again, beyond these, are the thousands of investors who from all parts of the world have sent their money to develop the South African Republic, and enrich the Boers themselves. In addition, there are the thousands of oppressed natives.

It is on behalf of these classes, then, that Her Majesty's Government should act, and quickly. Already, as we know, much valuable time has been lost, and more especially as, since the deplorable raid and Johannesburg fiasco, the Hollander has become master of the situation. No longer have we to deal only with stubborn and ignorant Boers. Clever unscrupulous foreigners now pull the strings, and life has been made intolerable to all outsiders by these greedy, money-grubbing cormorants. Daily, almost hourly, is some dull-witted lout on the Veldt roused to believe that what he holds so dear, his independence, is threatened by the hated "rooineck," and at any moment he may be urged to commit some rash act which will provoke a conflict.

The ordinary Boer on the Veldt to-day holds precisely the same narrow-minded religious views as did his father or grandfather, the Voortrekker. The black man, in his eyes, was born to be a hewer of wood and drawer of water, and on these lines he treats him, whilst the ever-to-be-condemned Englishman he regards as his natural antagonist. Lazy, shiftless, and dirty in his habits, but endowed with an abundant stock of cunning, he has greatly degenerated. The younger generation, too, have lost the accuracy of aim which distinguished their fathers, and the reason of this is because there is no longer any game.

Those multitudinous herds of different kinds of buck, from the diminutive klipspringer to the lordly eland, have vanished almost as rapidly as has the bison from the North American Continent. Consequently a Boer now neither needs, nor has he the opportunity of judging distances by firing at a moving object.

In spite of being provided with a rifle and ammunition at the expense of the Government, I maintain that the young Boers can shoot no better than an average squad of an English volunteer company. On more than one occasion I have seen a number fire in succession at a target, and they have been invariably beaten by Englishmen who entered into competition with them. I do not for a moment desire to disparage the shooting of Boers who learnt the art before the game disappeared. There are many of these still left skilled in the handling of a rifle, but when I am told that Boers generally are the best rifle shots in the world, I am bold enough to allege from my own experience that such a statement is absolute nonsense.

Another idea which seems to have taken hold of the public mind is that Witwatersrand is the only valuable portion of the South African Republic, but this is not accurate, for the narrow district of the Rand, which has suddenly jumped into prominence, is not by any means the only region where gold and other minerals are located. It is one section of the vast highly mineralised area of the Republic, but as this limited space has attracted a large portion of the surplus wealth of Europe, other parts have been comparatively neglected.

With their accustomed short-sightedness the Boers and Hollanders have come to regard the Rand, thanks to Uitlander enterprise, as the chief field in which to practise extortion, and at the same time they have placed every obstacle in the way of the development of any other district, though more favourably situated. So much so that legislative enactments have been largely directed against the rapidly growing alien population at this special centre. In their desire for greed they forgot that minerals form only a small portion of the country's assets, and that by frustrating railway communication and the building of roads and bridges, their obtuseness would affect the revenue and

prosperity of the entire community. Outside transport
riding, the Boers on the Veldt have only one occupation, agriculture, though carried out in a perfunctory
manner, and unless these men can carry their produce
to market their labour is valueless. Now what has
happened? Rinderpest, locusts, drought, and famine
have recently swept over the country—transport-riding
has gone. Cattle have vanished, horse-sickness has
prevailed, and the patient donkey is the only draught
animal to be relied on. Agriculture, therefore, cannot
be pursued unless railways are quickly built. Already
Mr. Rhodes has pushed his railway system from Cape
Town nearly to Buluwayo, thus rendering Rhodesia
independent of grain supplies from the South African
Republic, and of the route through the Transvaal, the
one which, from its shortness and easy gradients, has
hitherto enabled the Boers to control the traffic to
Charterland.

Instead of an enlightened perception of these
advantages, the Government officials at Pretoria place
every hindrance in the way of opening up their own
roads and markets, stifle the industry of their own
kith and kin, and prevent the Uitlander from develop-
ing the agricultural or mineral resources of the
Republic.

Would such a state of affairs be tolerated by any
civilised country? Take, for instance, the situation of
Johannesburg to-day. Here is a town containing
50,000 white inhabitants, who have to rely for their
supply of fruit, forage, vegetables, and meat on the
Cape Colony, Orange Free State, and Natal, and these
supplies have to be brought a distance of from 200 to

800 miles, whereas if railway communication were afforded, the entire city could obtain all its food requirements grown on Transvaal soil within a radius of 200 miles.

Imagine what this means to the Boer inhabitants alone, and setting aside consequent reduction of cost of living in Johannesburg itself.

I have taken this as an isolated instance, but the same doctrine applies to Pretoria and every other centre of population. Every human being knows that in all countries where a gold rush has attracted humanity, the ultimate prosperity of the country has been established by the necessity of feeding the persons engaged in that pursuit, and that as a rule the "Auri sacra fames" sinks into insignificance compared with the solid wealth acquired by the cultivation of the soil. Witness, in our own day, California and Australia.

So will it be in the Transvaal. Thousands of acres can be irrigated and brought under cultivation, and the produce thereof conveyed to market, showing a good margin of profit with which no outside territory can compete. Only roads and railways are required.

In the history of modern times, there is no picture so illustrative of what a few bold determined men can accomplish by the exercise of unlimited impudence, in the face of a great paramount Power, as that which the South African Republic now holds up to the world's view. For, be it recorded that the entire number who have controlled and brought about this condition of affairs have not exceeded in number more than fifty persons. This inner ring dominates the liberties and enjoyment of civil rights of more than 60,000 beings, many of them highly educated, and all resident in the country, sets at defiance Her Majesty as Suzerain, and laughs at her guarantee. Personally I must confess that I have a certain amount of respect for the audacity and dogged perseverance of President Kruger and his associates. His "holy humbug" has been the most powerful weapon in his armoury, and the only persons on whom his hypocritical cant has had no effect are the equally righteous Hollanders who now have Stephanus Johannis Paulus Kruger and his ignorant Boer Executive fairly in their grip.

In dealing with the present position, it must be remembered that no Boer in South Africa has displayed throughout his career such contempt for agitation by constitutional means as Paul Kruger. He has been in the thick of every fight, both as promoter and participant, whether against another section of his own race, or against the authority of the Crown, and had he not brought about a crisis by his deliberate violation of Uitlanders' rights, his manner and aggressive Dopper theological views would three years ago have landed Transvaal Boers in the throes of a sectarian civil war.

When a man has arrived at the firm belief that every act of his life is inspired by Divine Will—and this is the state of mental beatitude to which Mr. Kruger has brought himself—it is a somewhat difficult task to convince him that he can do wrong. Judging him by his own standard of ethics, we need not be surprised at the levity which he has displayed in tearing up any compact to which he had assented, when it stood in the way of his gaining his ends. Did not the Almighty direct Jacob in his transactions with Laban, when the latter had deceived him? And so to-day is not He guiding His Transvaal servant through the snares laid by evil-minded Rooinecks?

There is no better example afforded of President Kruger's patient determination to reach his goal and our weakness than that supplied by Swaziland. In the Conventions of 1881 and 1884, it was made a great feature that Swaziland was to remain independent of the Boers; and justly so, when our pledges to these natives are remembered, and their loyal behaviour to the Crown. Their adhesion to us, and propinquity to them, only excited the Boers, however, and covetous eyes were always cast by President Kruger and his Boer circle on Swazi territory. He knew that he had only to wait, play his cards properly, and the Swazis would drop into his hands like a ripe pear. By ceaseless representations, offers of liberality to Uitlanders within his borders since 1884, he at length wearied or humbugged Her Majesty's Government into handing over to his Boers the whole of Swaziland. But not content with this—for his ambition has ever been to extend the South African Republic to the sea-coast—he has made a bold attempt to get a grip on Amatongaland, and thus attain his long cherished desire. One can only marvel, considering the fate of all other Articles of these Conventions, that Her Majesty's advisers have not surrendered to the Republic this strip of littoral, "with a view to promote the peace and good order of the said State, and of the countries adjacent thereto."

Recollect that Paul Kruger's object is that of the old Voortrekker: the independence of the Boer race free from foreign interference, and anything which stands in the way of realising that ideal must be swept aside.

His last move to obtain a strong offensive and defensive alliance with the Orange Free State is only another part of his scheme to fuse South Africa under Boer control. What other interpretation, too, can be put on the offer to Free Staters of burgher rights in the Transvaal. He has persistently refused on all occasions to enter into any fair commercial union with the Colonies on the question of customs duties and railway tariffs. He and his Hollanders have been secretly intriguing with Germany to obtain German interference on behalf of the South African Republic, and numbers of military Germans have been recently imported into their service. Within the past twelve months more than one and a half millions sterling has been spent on arms, ammunition, and construction of forts, and £150,000 on secret service. During the same period President Kruger, in open violation of the Conventions, has caused his complaisant Raad to pass laws authorising the expulsion of aliens from the country without recourse to the Courts of Justice, muzzling the Press, compelling white immigrants to provide themselves with a pass, and, lastly, he has endeavoured to prevent the judges of the High Court from interpreting the law according to the Constitution.

But long before the Jameson raid, as we know, these Conventions were systematically broken, and as

Her Majesty's Government took no interest in the matter, save to truckle to the fifty Boers and Hollanders above mentioned, the Uitlander inhabitants of the country attempted to obtain justice for themselves. The story of that sad fiasco will long be remembered. But perhaps it will be convenient here to refresh our memories with some provisions of the Conventions which had been violated before those events occurred:

First, the franchise laws had been so modified as to exclude every alien for ever from acquiring burgher rights to the extent of giving him a vote to elect a member of the first Raad.

Secondly, monopolies had been created and concessions granted in direct opposition to Art. 14 of the Convention of 1884, which gives the right to "all persons to hire or possess houses, manufactories, warehouses, shops, and premises; they may carry on their commerce either in person, or by any agents whom they may think fit to employ."

Thirdly, the right of the alien to bring into the country all goods and merchandise on the same terms as the inhabitants of other States had been outraged by the closing of the drifts. Art. 13.

Fourthly, the enjoyment of all civil rights had been interfered with when the right of public meeting was withdrawn, and when the education of children of foreigners had to be conducted in Dutch.

Fifthly, taxes were levied on Uitlanders far heavier than on Boers in contravention of Article 14. In fact, every dodge that a grasping greedy group of extor-

M

tionists could practise to gain money had been resorted to.

But here I am constrained to state that I have no sympathy with those men who embarked on what is called the Jameson raid. A more foolish, impotent, harebrained enterprise was never undertaken. Every person interested in the Transvaal has suffered from this act of idiocy, the only effect of it having been to play into the hands of Boers and Hollanders, and enable them to aggravate the situation fifty-fold. It affords one no solatium to be told that, had the expedition proved successful, all would have benefited. From the outset, any man acquainted with the Transvaal outside Johannesburg must have known that success under the circumstances was a physical impossibility. No revolution of any kind should have been attempted without the overthrow of the present Boer Government being assured beyond the possibility of doubt. And I maintain, such was the feeling of trepidation amongst the Boer and Hollander clique just before the raid, when I was in Pretoria, that if Dr. Jameson's ill-starred expedition had not started, the Boer Government would not only have never passed their recent obnoxious and hurtful measures, but they would have granted many reforms which the Uitlanders then sought.

I have had a little personal experience of revolutions, having survived five in different republics, and I have travelled over a great part of the Transvaal, so that I am enabled to form some opinion of Boer military resources, of their ability to mobilise rapidly, and of the probable chances of conquest a force such as Jameson's might reasonably hope to possess. The Briton is not built for a revolutionist, unless he has been deeply wronged and his passions and patriotism are thoroughly roused, then he becomes dangerous. In this case, to aid the semi-disciplined youths who accompanied Jameson, there was in Johannesburg a comparatively unarmed cosmopolitan mob, without a leader to take the field, and divided in opinion even on the question of grievances. I firmly believe that five hundred resolute men, well mounted and armed, acting quickly and secretly, could then have seized Pretoria before the Boers had time to assemble. Another body of at least three thousand strong should have held Johannesburg, and all approaches by rail or road, and then Jameson's small force might have produced a considerable moral effect. But they had not the organisation, or the men, or the arms wherewith to do this; they neglected to strike, their supposed secrets were blabbed, and Mr. Kruger and his farmer friends only waited for "the tortoise to put out its head." We know the sequel, and what this rash folly has entailed, not only on residents and investors in Transvaal enterprises, but also on the residents and investors in Rhodesia. Had Dr. Jameson never crossed the border, in all probability we should have seen no Kaffir war, with its loss of life and concomitant horrors in Matabeleland and Mashonaland.

Besides, this untimely adventure seriously damaged the Uitlanders' cause in the eyes of those intelligent progressive Boers and burghers forming the minority in the First Raad, who for some time had manfully opposed Kruger and his Hollanders. Some alienated themselves entirely, while others maintained a circumspect silence, for fear their advocacy should be wilfully misinterpreted. Hence, since the raid, President Kruger has been able practically to stifle all opposition to his dictatorial commands.

In common fairness, however, both to Dr. Jameson and his followers, and to the leaders of the so-called revolt in Johannesburg, we should not forget that the rising had been entirely provoked by President Kruger and his Government. Petitions and remonstrances, instead of producing a beneficial effect, were treated at Pretoria with ridicule and contumely. Moreover, Her Majesty's Government maintained that discreet reserve for which they are famous when British interests in South Africa are imperilled, so that at last, goaded by tyranny and insult of every kind, they were driven to take this foolish step without due provision or preparation.

But these errors or mistakes, or what they have subsequently brought in their train, have only rendered it more imperative on Her Majesty's Government to take action now. They were the sinners when Mr. Gladstone and his colleagues, through Lord Kimberley, in 1881, gave the Boers to understand it was no part of the policy of Her Majesty's Government to extend British territory in South Africa, and afterwards, when in 1884 they wilfully eliminated from the Convention the main conditions which Her Majesty as Suzerain had imposed, so as to guarantee complete self-government to all inhabitants of the Transvaal State.

It is most difficult to write on any subject connected with South Africa without bringing into prominence the name of Mr. Rhodes, the man so pre-eminently associated both with its immediate past, present, and future. I do not propose to add much to the many reams which have been written of and about this gentleman. I have never spoken to Mr. Rhodes in my life, I have never held a share in the Chartered Company or in any Rhodesian enterprise or in any concern with which his name is connected, so that any opinion which I may have formed respecting him and his works cannot be ascribed, as is the fashion nowadays, to pecuniary influence.

Without hesitation then, I state that I look on Mr. Rhodes as being one of the greatest of living Englishmen. Mistakes he has made, and he has frankly admitted them. He has acquired immense wealth, and has not used it to gratify his own selfish pleasures, but as a means to carry out one of the boldest and most colossal enterprises which the brain of an ambitious man ever conceived.

What, may one ask, would have been the position of Cape Colony to-day, with the fortunes of which he has allied himself, without Mr. Rhodes? And what about these extensions of British colonial possessions of which our politicians now express themselves to be so proud! Is it nothing to have, within ten years, occupied for the Crown, rescued from barbarism and opened up to trade, a stretch of country equal in extent to the area of France and Germany? Is it nothing to have pushed through British territory railway communication, which, according to Sir James Siveright, no mean authority, will enable Cape Colony to pay six per cent. on twenty millions sterling, even if the traffic through the Orange Free State fails ?   Is it nothing that this man has done more than any other person living to conciliate the Dutch and English races in South Africa, so as to weld them in one firm bond as loyal subjects of Her Majesty ?

That Mr. Rhodes is fit to rank with the bravest, his recent conduct testifies, as witness his courageous entry into the Matoppo Hills to pacify a horde of savage Kaffirs, and to stop further bloodshed.   And that he is merciful and forgiving, his instructions to Lord Grey to buy up to £50,000 worth of mealies on his responsibility, and distribute them amongst the starving natives, bears silent but eloquent tribute.

Compare this man and his policy with that of Mr. Gladstone and his Ministers in 1881, before you attempt to pass judgment on him !

Take up the map of Africa at that date and look at the rich country then under the protection of the Crown, which they have since surrendered to the Boers, despite the Conventions, then place that map alongside the map of Africa of to-day and see how much territory Mr. Rhodes has added to the Empire.   And whilst you do this, may those memorable words ring in your ears, written by Lord Kimberley in 1881, when Mr. Gladstone's Cabinet were preparing to leave all British subjects, white or black indiscriminately, to their fate : " Her Majesty's Government are averse on general grounds of policy to the extension of British territory in South Africa."

The name of Mr. Rhodes is in all men's mouths, and

how he was adding to and consolidating the Empire whilst these valiant Little Englanders were trying their utmost to disintegrate it, is matter of common knowledge.

It is my humble opinion that in the time to come, when the eminent personages who formed Mr. Gladstone's Ministry in 1881 and 1884 have become a lingering memory, the name of Mr. Rhodes will be oft recalled with pride by young and old, dwellers in the land which bears his name, and still further beyond the seas, wherever the English language is spoken, he will be remembered as one of the best and bravest of the "old Lion's whelps."

Instead of being antagonistic to the South African Republic, I feel assured that Mr. Rhodes has all along laboured to bring the Transvaal Boers to consent to an honest commercial union on the question of customs and railway tariffs, and it was only in 1894, at an interview with President Kruger, where the latter lost his temper and expressed himself in violent terms, that Mr. Rhodes felt his task to be absolutely impossible.

Some opinion of the ingratitude of this Boer and Hollander ring, and their machinations, may be formed from Mr. Rhodes's evidence on March 5th, before the Parliamentary Committee, and I assert that a man who could not be influenced by such considerations would be superhuman.

"You said in your evidence on Tuesday, in answer to Mr. Bigham, that you believed the Netherlands Railway was practically only in name an independent railway ?—Yes.

"You understood the Government controlled it ?—Yes.

"I wish to ask you whether the policy on that railway during the year 1896 was resented by Cape Colony ?—You mean in reference to raising their rates upon us and also the difficulties they threw in the way of our traffic ?

"Yes ?—I remember a telegram of Sir James Siveright, who was in our Cabinet. It was dated June 13 and was sent to the manager of the Netherlands Company. He said, 'My sole object is to urge you that this colony is not receiving that fair treatment which I maintain it has a right, according to solemn treaty obligations, to expect in handling of its traffic with South African Republic.' And then, of course, after that we had the trouble of the raising of the carriage. After we had lent them the money they put the tariff up so much. I must point out that actually when they raised the tariff against us it was an infringement of the arrangement between the Raad and the Netherlands Company. When the Raad gave the Netherlands Company their concession they naturally put in a schedule of the upper limit of charges. Then in order to shut our trade out they charged a tariff in excess of that which had been arranged, and Kruger actually sanctioned this increased tariff against British goods, which was raised by the Netherlands Company against us, and that of course caused tremendous friction.

"Then the President had to intervene to enable the company to put its rates up ?—Exactly.

"And without his intervention the company would

not under its contract have been able to put them up?
—No, because the rates were beyond the tariff arranged
by the State, and the arrangement to allow us to come
into the State was nominally with the Netherlands
Company. I remember there was a report in 1894. It
showed that the total importations to the Transvaal were
in March 1894—*viâ* Cape Colony 75 per cent., *viâ* Natal
15 per cent., and *viâ* Delagoa 9 per cent. In April
1894, however, under the embarrassments created by
the Netherlands Company these importations were—*viâ*
Cape Colony 62 per cent., *viâ* Natal 18 per cent., and
viâ Delagoa 18 per cent.

" This was going on some time ?—Yes. But we also
had checks and difficulties in connection with the traffic,
and afterwards came our heavy differences with them
when they raised the rates.

" This heavy difference, as you call it, arose, did it
not, when the Delagoa Bay line was opened in that
year, 1894 ?—Yes.

" That was the occasion for putting up these rates ?
—Yes.

" I see that Sir James Siveright expostulated. Did
you take any measures in that year to resent this policy
of the Netherlands Railway, a policy which was only
made possible, as you told us, by the President ?—
When I came down from the north I came to Delagoa
Bay and called at Pretoria and saw the President, and
I told him it was contrary to the spirit of our agreement that he should go and raise the rates beyond the
rates allowed by the Raad, and he said he had the
right to do it. I said, ' This is really breaking the spirit
of the convention.' I said, ' It is most unfair, we lent

you £700,000 when you could get it from no one else, and the result of that was that the Rothschilds lent you a million and a half to complete the Delagoa Bay line, and as soon as you have got that you break the spirit of this convention and raise the rates against us.' I said, 'If you do not look out you will have the whole of South Africa against you; you are a very strong man, but there are feelings aroused against you in Cape Colony, in the north, and the feeling of your own people is so strongly against you that you will not be able to stand against them.' I warned him very clearly.

"That was in 1894?—Yes.

"And as a matter of fact those rates were not enforced in 1894?—They were in 1895.

"They were enforced on January 1, 1895?—Yes.

Another attack on Uitlander rights in 1895 roused the indignation of the entire South African community. This was the closing of the Drifts on the frontier of the Orange Free State. For some time, mine-owners and merchants at Johannesburg had been driven by the extortions of Mr. Kruger and his Hollanders to have their goods carried from the Vaal River by ox-waggon in competition with the Netherlands Railway, so he proceeded to close the roads against that means of transport, only admitting produce from the Orange Free State to pass through. This procedure was such an outrageous violation of the Conventions that Her Majesty's Government at last put its foot down, and the strong remonstrances from the Colonial Office had the desired effect. President Kruger withdrew his proclamation.

Recently, with commendable promptness, Her Majesty's Government has decided to strengthen our garrisons in South Africa, and the firm attitude of Mr. Chamberlain has already brought about, within the past few days, one salutary result at any rate.

Finding that we are in earnest and do not intend to shirk our national responsibilities, the Volksraad at Pretoria has been induced to repeal one of the most obnoxious laws recently passed, the Act affecting immigrants, and this too by a vote of twenty against three. It is fair to assume, therefore, that when further pressure is brought to bear, other measures which have been sanctioned, flagrantly violating Articles of the Convention, will also be repealed. But vigilance must not be relaxed. Above all, outside arbitration as to what constitutes an infraction of an Article cannot be entertained. The issues involved in the faithful observance of the Articles substituted in 1884 are so simple and so obvious that no arbitration on any point is necessary. Those Articles were for the benefit of all, and cannot be overridden or set aside by a vindictive minority for their own ends. But even if the occasion for arbitration on any question should arise to which these articles relate, Her Majesty as Suzerain can be the only arbitrator, inasmuch as all disputes must be between one section of the inhabitants and another; and the section feeling itself aggrieved can rightfully call on the Suzerain to decide their differences and enforce Her guarantee against the offender.

Let Her Majesty's Government adopt the same

firmness in every other direction where Articles of the Convention have been similarly ruthlessly broken. If this be done, we shall be treated to a good many pious ejaculations and canting allusions to the Old Testament no doubt, but the Boer Hollander coterie will adopt a different tone very quickly. They are perfectly conversant with the fact that their recent high-handed outrages of decency have estranged from them the sympathy of the British and French public now so largely interested in the Transvaal, and they have arrived at the conclusion that although the German Emperor may send frothy telegrams, he dare not move a man to aid them against the Suzerain authority in South Africa. President Kruger has had ample opportunities of learning what is the power of England should her strength be put forth, and if he once sees we are in earnest, he will give way. It behoves Her Majesty's advisers, however, to remember that there is at this hour as much difference between his promises and his performances as there was at the time he was treating either with Mr. Gladstone's Cabinet, British officials and the Royal Commissioners, or when he was Commandant-General in Zoutpansberg.

What reason then can be alleged for further delay? Is it not a hard petrified fact that the Articles of the Conventions have been openly defied? Does not the whole world know that the administration of justice has been reduced to a mere mockery and farce, the personal liberty and rights of some 60,000 aliens imperilled, and millions of capital invested in the Transvaal endangered by a few dishonest and illiterate peasants, assisted by a batch of still more unscrupulous foreign Dutch?

Let Her Majesty's Government continue to strengthen our military forces at all strategic points, and show the Boers that at last Great Britain is serious, and if need be that Her Majesty's guarantee will be enforced by Her Majesty's troops. Then I feel sure the game or bluff will cease, wiser councils will prevail, war will be averted and reforms granted satisfactory to all parties. But these steps must be taken promptly. Remember that the terrible mistakes made over a series of years are not to be corrected in a day, and that each of these ignorant farmers on the Veldt has the idea firmly impressed in his mind that on more than one occasion the Boers have vanquished the entire British power. To those not interested, the position must appear farcical, but any day the farce may develop into tragedy, and only a prompt resolute stand taken by the Suzerain can avert bloodshed.

APPENDIX

Sir T. SHEPSTONE, K.C.M.G., *to the* EARL OF CARNARVON.
(*Received May 26,* 1877.)

GOVERNMENT HOUSE, PRETORIA, TRANSVAAL,
April 17, 1877.

MY LORD,

On Thursday last, the 12th instant, I found myself in a position to issue the proclamations necessary for annexing the South African Republic, commonly known as the Transvaal, to Her Majesty's dominions, and for assuming the administration thereof in virtue of the powers conferred upon me by Her Majesty's Commission, dated Balmoral, the 5th day of October, 1876. I enclose printed copies of these two proclamations, and my address to the people, for your Lordship's information, and, I hope, approval. These documents describe the considerations which chiefly induced me to take this step. The facts showing the perilous and utterly deplorable condition of the Government and country could, with perfect truth, have been stated in much stronger language; indeed, they had been more strongly stated by Mr. Burgers himself in speeches addressed to the Volksraad by him as President, extracts from which I have used in my address to the people.

2. Every step I have taken towards the accomplishment of my object was taken with the knowledge of the President. I thought it my duty to be perfectly open and frank with him

from the beginning, and on the last occasion of my meeting him in Executive Council he took the opportunity to acknowledge and thank me for what he was good enough to call my considerate and frank behaviour to him and the Government.

3. After this meeting, and in compliance with a request made thereat, I addressed the letter of the 9th April (copy annexed) informing Mr. Burgers of my intention. He subsequently called upon me, and informed me that he should be bound to make a protest, the draft of which he read to me. I agreed with Mr. Burgers, that from his point of view he could take no other course, and you will observe that the wording of the protest is as moderate as was compatible with the object it was intended to attain.

4. On Wednesday, the 11th instant, the Attorney-General and Chief Clerk came and officially read the protest to me, and at the same time handed in a resolution of the Executive Council (copy of each herewith enclosed), from which it appeared that in addition to the protest a mission to Her Majesty's Government, and contingently to other Governments which had acknowledged the independence of the State, had been determined upon. The resolution appointed the Attorney-General, E. J. P. Jorissen, LL.D., and Mr. Paul Kruger, Vice-President, to be members of this mission, with power to add a third person, if required. I received these papers, but as they contained nothing to induce me to change the view I had taken of my duty, I said that while I recognised the propriety of their discharging what they conceived to be incumbent upon them, I must ask them to do the same with regard to me; they expressed their acquiescence, and the interview, which had been friendly throughout, ended.

5. Mr. Burgers called upon me shortly afterwards and explained to me the object of these documents.

6. The following day, at 11 A.M., Mr. Osborne, Secretary of the mission, accompanied by seven other gentlemen of my staff, whose names appear on the margin, walked down to Church Square, and in front of the public offices read my proclamations to a small crowd of the inhabitants, mostly English, by whom, of course, the most hearty cheers were given for Her Majesty. Mr. Burgers' protest and proclamation

were immediately afterwards read by Mr. Juta, one of the members of the Executive Government, and were received in respectful silence. No excitement whatever followed.

7. Mr. Burgers' proclamation, translation of which I enclose, informed the people that the Government had decided to submit under protest, mentioned the intention to send a mission to Europe, and called upon all Government officers, burghers, and other inhabitants to avoid violent word or deed whereby the mission might be rendered fruitless ; and, on the contrary, exhorted them to assist in carrying out the decision of the Government and in the maintenance of order.

8. Every effort had been made during the previous fortnight by, it is said, educated Hollanders residing at the seat of Government, and who had but lately arrived in the country, to rouse the fanaticism of the Boers, and to induce them to offer " bloody " resistance to what it was known I intended to do. The Boers were appealed to in the most inflammatory language by printed manifestoes and memorials; agents were sent out to excite them by violent speeches at public meetings, and every possible means were used to intimidate individuals and stifle the expression of real opinion; it was urged that I had but a small escort, which could easily be overpowered, and that there would be no difficulty in putting the mission across the border; but, as I had judged from the first, the daily accumulating pressure and personal distress which the circumstances of the country were bringing upon them had created in the minds of the people a conviction that the State did not possess inherent vitality enough to relieve them, and that the only prospect of relief lay in accepting my proposal. Every intelligent man, from the highest to the lowest, with whom I discussed the question frankly admitted this, and those who opposed my mission because of their positions in the State were equally frank in the expression in that direction of their personal opinions. I know, therefore, that in spite of the efforts to create opposition there was at bottom no feeling strong enough to nourish it; and my judgment has been so far confirmed by the fact that from the moment that the pro- clamation was published to this, opposition has been gradually dying away and the disposition to accept the situation growing apace.

N

9 Immediately after the issue of the proclamation Mr. Burgers addressed the assembled officials, and, in taking leave of them, urged them to loyally serve the new Government. He directed Mr. Swart, the State Secretary, to hand over formally to me the key of the offices, a direction which he (Mr. Swart) at once came to the house I occupy to comply with, and upon his doing so I handed it back to his charge.

10. The officers of the late Republic, including every member of the Executive Council except Mr. Paul Kruger, one of the delegates appointed to go to Europe, have all signified in writing their willingness to serve under the new form of Government. There has not been time for the notification of the intentions of the Landdrosts and others in charge of districts at a distance to reach me, but I have good reason to believe that all will follow the example of their officers at the seat of Government.

11. With regard to the protest and the points urged in the minute of the Executive Council I have very little to say. My proclamation and address to the people show clearly the state of the country, and the impossibility of my leaving it without at once precipitating its destruction, first, by the anarchy and civil war it would at once have produced, and, next, by the attacks from natives which that anarchy would at once have invited. I dared not, therefore, entertain such a thought. None of the points urged by the Executive Council are left unanswered in the documents I have issued; none show the existence of any hope in the Councillors themselves that the country could raise itself by means within itself from its depressed condition, and they afford no certain prospect for the future, except the annihilation of the State and the placing of all the white communities of South Africa in the utmost peril.

12 The protest, the minute and decision of the Executive Council, as well as the proclamation by Mr. Burgers, were necessary to calm strong feelings here and there, but the great value of them has been that of furnishing an excuse to the great body of the people to accept quietly what they feel is the only means of saving themselves and the country.

13. In the resolution or minute of the Executive Council

my act is described as one of " violence." It seems to me to be necessary only to state that the Transvaal is about the same size as Great Britain and Ireland put together; that it is believed to contain a population of 40,000 whites and 800,000 natives; that I entered this territory with my personal staff only, and an escort of 25 Natal mounted policemen, on 4th January, and, after slow progress, reached Pretoria, the capital, on 22nd January last; that I have never hesitated, during these three months and more, to explain to both the Government and the people the condition of the State, and the only remedy that appeared to me capable of saving it from immediate ruin; that I have again and again expressed my willingness to at once withdraw, if any plan, or action, or latent power in the country could be shown me by which its independence could be maintained, and the danger to its neighbours be averted, but without result; that I have invariably been, and still am, treated with the utmost deference and respect by all classes of the people; and that the only means by which I could have used violence in carrying out what I have done—*i.e.*, Her Majesty's troops—were four weeks' march from me, in the colony of Natal, and cannot be here, even now, within a fortnight, or very nearly a month after the issue of my proclamation, and of my having assumed the Government. These facts will, I think, show your lordship conclusively that I have acted in accordance with the real convictions and feelings of the people, and that, for an officer, accompanied as I was, by a staff of twelve gentlemen, and an escort of twenty-five men, openly and avowedly to attempt to subvert the government of a country, and place himself at its head against the true wishes of such a people, would have been an act of madness.

14. There is also another expression in the same document, regarding which I wish to make a few remarks. The natives are spoken of as a "common enemy" to the whites; this may have been the case in the Transvaal under its late form of government, and the history of past transactions with the coloured races will probably support this view, but I desire to state my conviction, earnestly and deliberately based upon an experience of forty-two years' duration, that this need not be the case, and will not be the case under Her Majesty's

rule; that these people are, as compared with the Zulu race, unwarlike, and inclined to peaceful industry; that, in their readiness to adopt civilised ideas and habits, they are also unlike the Zulus, who are a proud, conservative people, and are naturally opposed to the encroachments of civilisation.

15. I feel sure that there will be but little difficulty in ruling the large native population which this country contains; justice and firmness, a conviction that their wrongs will be righted, and their rights protected, will make them good and obedient subjects, and open to philanthropists a door to their benevolent operations that will lead them more safely and easily to Central Africa than any base of action that has hitherto been open to them.

16. To avoid all unnecessary irritation, I thought it best to defer the formal raising of the flag until the arrival of the troops, when the act can be accompanied by becoming and necessary formalities; in the meanwhile the republican flag has ceased to be hoisted, and the Union Jack flies from the flag-staff at the house which I occupy.

I have, &c.,

(Signed)   T. SHEPSTONE,
Her Majesty's Special Commissioner and Administrator
of the Transvaal Government.

THE RIGHT HON. THE EARL OF CARNARVON, &c. &c.

P. S.—I have not had time to offer any explanations regarding the different points in my proclamation annexing the country, upon which I have, upon suggestions made to me, pledged the faith of Her Majesty's Government. I shall endeavour to do so at an early opportunity.

(Signed)   T. S.

(Translation.)

RESOLUTION *of the Executive Council, dated the* 11*th of April,* 1877.—ART. 7.

ON THE ORDER,

DESPATCH from Her British Majesty's Special Commissioner, dated the 9th of April 1877, giving notice that his Excellency has decided to proclaim without delay British authority over the South African Republic. It is resolved :—

That whereas Her British Majesty's Government, by the Convention of Sand River, 1852, has solemnly pledged the independence of the people to the north of the Vaal River, and that whereas the Government of the South African Republic is not aware of ever having given any reason for a hostile action on the part of Her Majesty's Government, nor any grounds for such an act of violence.

That whereas this Government has ever shown its readiness, and is still prepared, to do all which in justice and equity may be demanded, and also to remove all causes of dissatisfaction that may exist. Whereas also the Government has repeatedly expressed its entire willingness to enter into such treaties or agreements with Her Majesty's Government as may be considered necessary for the general protection of the white population of South Africa, and is prepared punctually to execute such agreements: And whereas according to public statements of Her Majesty's Secretary of State for the Colonies, Lord Carnarvon, there exists no desire on the part of the British Government to force the people of the South African Republic against their wish under the authority of the British Government: And whereas the people, by memorials or otherwise, have by a large majority plainly stated that they are averse to it: And whereas this Government is aware that it is not in a condition to maintain the rights and independence of the people with the sword against the superior power of Great Britain, and, moreover, has no desire in any way to take any steps by which the white inhabitants of South Africa would be divided, in the face of the common enemy, against each other, or might come in hostile contact with each other, to the great danger of the entire Christian population of South Africa, without having first employed all means to secure in a peaceful way and by friendly mediation the rights of the people, therefore the Government protests most strongly against this act of Her Majesty's Special Commissioner.

It is also further resolved to send without delay a commission of delegates to Europe and America, with full power and instruction to add to their number a third person if required, in order to endeavour, in the first place, to lay before Her Majesty's Government the desire and wishes of the people, and in case this might not have the desired effect, which this Government would deeply regret, and cannot as yet believe, then to appeal to the friendly assistance and intercession of other Powers, particularly of those who have acknowledged the independence of this State. As members of this Commission are appointed the Honourable the Attorney-General, Dr. E. J. P. Jorissen, and S. J. P. Kruger, Vice-President of the South African Republic.

PROCLAMATION.

(*Translation.*)

WHEREAS Her British Majesty's Special Commissioner, Sir Theophilus Shepstone, in spite of my solemn protest presented yesterday against his Excellency's intention, communicated to me by letter, dated 9th April, has thought fit to carry out that intention, and has this day proclaimed the authority of Her British Majesty's Government over the South African Republic.

And whereas the Government has in the first place resolved to submit under protest, in order meanwhile to send a mission, in the persons of the Honourable S. J. P. Kruger and E. P. Jorissen, to Europe and America, in order thus to defend the rights of the people, and to endeavour in a peaceable way to settle the matter:

So it is that I, Thomas François Burgers, State President of the South African Republic, by this, in the name and by the advice of the Executive Council, command all officials, burghers, and inhabitants to refrain from any word or deed of violence whereby the mission may be made fruitless. And I exhort all burghers and inhabitants to help, maintain, and support the resolutions of the Government for the preservation of order and the prevention of bloodshed.

(Signed)   THOS. BURGERS,
State President.

GOVERNMENT OFFICE, PRETORIA,

   12th April, 1877.

LETTER FROM MR. KRUGER.

(*Translation.*)

KAALFONTEIN, *November* 29, 1880.

SIR,

   I BEG to inform you herewith that I have submitted an account of our interview of this morning to the assembled people.

We have agreed upon holding a general meeting of the people on 8th December next.

I hope and trust, as I informed you and as you agreed to, that the Government will place no obstacle in the way by summonses, writs of execution, or any military movements.

Should it happen, however, that movements are taken on your part, I must distinctly inform you I shall not be responsible for the consequences.

I have, &c.,

(Signed)   S. J. P. KRUGER.

The Honourable G. HUDSON,
   Government Secretary.

Mr. HUDSON'S ANSWER TO Mr. KRUGER'S LETTER.

POTCHEFSTROOM, *November* 30, 1880.

SIR,

   I HAVE the honour to acknowledge the receipt of your letter of yesterday's date received by me at 1.25 P.M. to-day.

I clearly placed before the committee my contention that no Government worthy of the name would submit to be called upon to suspend the operation of the law. In the form in which you placed matters before me, you threw upon the Government the responsibility of what might arise from any precipitate action on its part. The Government is fully aware of and prepared to accept the responsibility of its course of action.

Major Clarke has now been appointed Special Commissioner for the district of Potchefstroom, to whom further correspondence if necessary may be addressed.

I have, &c.,

(Signed)   GEORGE HUDSON,
Colonial Secretary.

S. J. PAUL KRUGER, Esq.,
Kaalfontein.

REPORT OF Mr. HUDSON, *Colonial Secretary to His Excellency* Sir OWEN LANYON, K.C.M.G., C.B.

POTCHEFSTROOM, *December* 1, 1880

YOUR EXCELLENCY,

Following my letters of the 26th and 28th ultimo, I have the honour to report that Potchefstroom is still in a disturbed state, and the inhabitants appear to view matters as critical. On Monday I left this at 8 A.M. for Kaalfontein to meet Mr. Paul Krüger and Boer Committee. I took with me only a special constable named Ribas, who drove me. I may here mention that on Friday last Captain Raaf went out to notify, if he should desire it, my willingness to meet Mr. Krüger, and was rather roughly handled, being met some distance from the laager, searched, and an attempt was made to lead him and his horse in. On his return he told me that he thought at one time they would have seized and kept him there, and he did not care to advise me to go out. I told him I must go according to arrangement.

The Boer laager is about twenty miles from here. When about two miles from it an escort of two men met us and took us into camp, where I should say about 400 men were gathered. Ribas informs me he counted 618 horses and mules, but there were many more.

I met with a very sullen reception, and Mr. Paul Krüger appeared nervous and very anxious that I should keep out of sight of the "volk" (people) as much as possible. Mr. Krüger then took me into a room, where a meeting between about ten persons and myself took place. The interview here began:—

MR. KRUGER: I hurried down from Rustenburg hearing that matters were serious, but I now find them more so than I expected. In fact, I don't know what to think of it. The committee had been working with the people, and arrangements had been made for a meeting on 9th January 1881, and now the Government has upset the whole thing. I and others are now doing our best for a peaceable arrangement, but if the Government precipitates matters I will wash my hands of all responsibility.

MR. HUDSON: I have come here to meet Mr. Krüger with a like object, and I think I can claim to have the best interests of the country at heart. I am a colonist, and came up here in the hope that I might promote South African interests. I am equally anxious with Mr. Krüger to assist in preventing any disturbance, and would strongly urge upon those for whom warrants are out to surrender and trust themselves to the mercy of the Government.

MR. KRÜGER: Why, when the people are protesting, and a meeting notified for 9th January, which the committee are trying to make pass off peaceably, does the Government worry them by tax collecting, executions, &c. The Government should have waited till then.

MR. HUDSON: Surely, Mr. Krüger, you cannot suppose that any Government would consent to suspend the operation of the law because of some meeting that was supposed to be held. The law must take its course.

MR. KRUGER: The Government has precipitated matters, the people are impatient, and matters are now serious. Had the Government waited, the committee would have laid before the people on 9th January Mr. Gladstone's proposals, and have been prepared to have taken action on them, and matters peaceably arranged.

MR. HUDSON: The Government has received no information from the committee of the object of the meeting, or any intimation that any proposals from Mr. Gladstone had been received, or were to be discussed; at least I never heard of it.

MR. KRÜGER: Everything has been published, so that every one might read what was going on, and so long as the people protested the Government should not harass them.

MR. HUDSON: As I have said before, the Government cannot suspend any of its legitimate functions. As regards the collection of taxes, why should one pay and not another? As a Government we are merely carrying out the laws of the country.

MR. BODENSTEIN: Why should taxes not be allowed to be received under protest till this meeting?

MR. HUDSON: Because I never yet heard of a Government receiving taxes under a protest, such as you propose; it could not do so. It might lead you to entertain the idea that if the country were given back the money would have to be returned to you by the British Government.

MR. KRÜGER: It is not the British Government, or the English people, it is acts of the Government and the misrepresentations of Sir Bartle Frere, Wolseley, and Lanyon that have brought matters to this state.

MR. HUDSON: I am not aware of any act of this Government which could justify the present defiance to law and order, and as to the alleged misrepresentations, I do not understand what is meant.

MR. CRONJÉ: Are you aware of what took place between Bezuidenhout and the Landdrost of Potchefstroom, and all the circumstances which have led to the present difficulties?

MR. HUDSON: I am not aware of the particulars; the Government is under the impression that everything has been done according to law, if any injustice has been done to Mr. Bezuidenhout, he has redress by law, or a representation to Government. When I get back to Pretoria I will make inquiries, though, as I have intimated, he could appeal to a higher court.

MR. CRONJÉ: I would like to state the case. Mr. Bezuidenhout was served with a tax notice to pay £27 5s. He appeared at the office of the Landdrost of Potchefstroom, and told him he was willing to pay £14, which was all that could legally be demanded. The Landdrost refused to receive it, but said Bezuidenhout must pay £27 5s., but he declined to do so. He was then summoned for £27 5s., and appeared, presenting his last receipts, and tendered again £14. The Landdrost answered as before. Bezuidenhout flatly refused to pay. Subsequently judgment was given for £14 with £8 costs, and the waggon was attached for the £14. If this matter is looked into, it will be seen how illegally the Govern· has acted.

MR. HUDSON : The Government is not aware of the case as you have stated it, and I cannot say more than I have already said.

MR. FONCHÉ: Why did the Government adopt such an unusual course as to send troops down to execute the arrest ?

MR. HUDSON : There was not a single soldier sent down or used to carry out the process of the law. Special constables only were used, and they were resisted.

MR. BODENSTEIN: Why were no summonses issued in the usual way ? Had that been done, the present difficulties would not have occurred ; the troops coming down made the difficulty.

MR. HUDSON : I understand from Mr. Cronjé that summonses were issued, but that is a judicial matter, and if any wrong has been done, it can be righted in the usual way. I have come to urge you to settle matters quietly, and hope you will urge upon those for whom warrants are out to give themselves up ; these points are only personal ones.

MR. KRÜGER: Why, while the people are protesting generally, do the Government try to stop them ? The committee were working for peace, and do not want bloodshed, and if the Government had allowed the people's committee to act it might have been different. Even now, the Government have arrested the printer, Mr. Celliers, who published their protests ; why did the Government do that ? Matters have arrived at the state now that I do not know how much further they will go (here a member or person in the room said to Mr. Krüger, " Yes you do, or else you know," and put his hands round his neck, indicating as I understood, that he would, have a halter round his neck).

Mr. Hudson : The Government has never interfered with the peaceful efforts or intentions of the committee.   Surely the Government has a right as much as private persons to take notice of defamatory articles.   The courts and the laws of the country will decide whether Mr. Celliers or the Government is right, so I don't see that any person can object to an appeal to them, if disposed to make it.

Mr. Krüger : The people are a protesting people, and should not be hindered in their words.

Mr. Hudson : Is there anything you wish me to convey to the Government ?

Mr. Krüger : We must now speak to the people, it is their matter, and we can do nothing.   I came to prevent bloodshed, and to shorten the time of the meeting, and wrote a letter to the Landdrost, with our minutes, which have not been forwarded.

Mr. Hudson : Will you let me have a copy ?

Mr. Krüger : No, I cannot give you a copy, it is of no use, they are cancelled.   The Government has taken its course, issued summonses, writs, and brought troops, and I must let the people now decide.   We are now calling them up, and will determine what we will do ; but if the Government interferes or does anything to exasperate them, I wash my hands of all responsibility.

Mr. Hudson : The Government is equally anxious with yourself for a satisfactory settlement of this matter.   As you are calling the people up the matter will now soon be settled. I can say no more than to express my earnest hope that the decision you arrive at will be the right one.

Here the interview ended.

I was escorted back for about one mile from the laager by three mounted Boers.

On Tuesday I received the enclosed letter from Mr. Paul Krüger, to which I sent a reply.   (Copy herewith.)

The political results which would appear to have arisen out of this case require, I think, that Government should inves-tigate it.   I have, &c.,

(Signed) GEORGE HUDSON,
Colonial Secretary.

His Excellency Sir Owen Lanyon, K.C.M.G., C.B.

Instructions.

The Right Hon. the EARL OF KIMBERLEY *to* Sir HERCULES ROBINSON, G.C.M.G.

DOWNING STREET, *March* 31, 1881.

SIR,

You have received from Sir Evelyn Wood a statement of the conditions agreed upon between him and the leaders of the Transvaal Boers on the 21st March, and I have now the honour to acquaint you that the Queen has approved of the appointment of yourself, Sir E. Wood, and Sir H. de Villiers to be Her Majesty's Commissioners for considering and advising upon the final agreements for the settlement of the affairs of the Transvaal.

I shall shortly transmit to you a Commission under the Queen's sign manual and signet for the appointment of the Commissioners, but as the first duties of the Commissioners will be those of inquiry and discussion, and some time must elapse before any formal action on their part will be required, the Commission will have been able to enter without delay upon the consideration of the matter referred to it. You will preside at the meetings of the Commission, and in your absence Sir E. Wood has precedence of Sir H. de Villiers.

I have communicated to President Brand by telegraph the hope of Her Majesty's Government that he will be able to be present, as representing a friendly State, at the proceedings of the Royal Commission, and I understand that he proposes to apply to the Volksraad for the leave necessary to enable him to go beyond the Free State for that purpose.

It has been agreed that the Commissioners should meet such representatives as the Boers may select to express their views, and should fully discuss with them the questions which have to be settled.

The Commissioners will make such arrangements for the time and place of their meetings as may be most convenient to all parties.

It may be desirable that the Commission should in the first instance address itself to the principal points referred to in the general terms of settlement agreed to by Sir E. Wood with the Boer leaders, a summary of which is contained in his telegram to me of the 21st March,* and to some extent further explained in subsequent telegraphic correspondence. I may recapitulate them briefly, as follows:

The Transvaal State is to enjoy complete self-government under the suzerainty of the Queen; the control of its relations with foreign Powers being reserved to the British Government.

A British Resident may be appointed at the capital of the Transvaal State, with such functions as Her Majesty's Government may determine on the recommendation of the Commission.

The Commission is to consider provisions for the protection of native interests.

The Commission is further to consider whether any portion, within certain limits, mentioned in my telegram to Sir E. Wood, of March 17,† should be severed from the country now included in the Transvaal Province.

There is to be no molestation for political opinion either way, and a complete amnesty is to be accorded to all who have taken part in the present war, excepting only persons who have committed or are directly responsible for acts contrary to the rules of civilised warfare.

Immunity from civil process is guaranteed to the Boer leaders individually and collectively for acts done in reference to the war until self-government is accorded, and the question of compensation to either side for acts not justified by necessities of war is remitted to the Commission to judge what acts were justified.

Besides these principal points there are some other matters referred to in the agreement entered into by Sir E. Wood, as reported in his telegrams to me, and there are further points not mentioned by him which will have to be provided for in the final settlement. Of the latter the most important are the determination of a boundary line in the territory known as the Keate Award, the payment of the public debt of the Province and the recognition of all lawful acts done by the

* No. 123 of [C. 2837] March 1881.
† No. 115 of [C. 2837] March 1881.

Government during the British occupation. I will deal in order with the various points to which I have referred.

Entire freedom of action will be accorded to the Transvaal Government so far as is not inconsistent with the rights expressly reserved to the suzerain Power. The term suzerainty has been chosen as most conveniently describing superiority over a State possessing independent rights of government subject to reservations with reference to certain specified matters.

The most material of these reserved rights is the control of the external relations of the future Transvaal State, which will be vested in the British Government, including, of course, the conclusion of treaties and the conduct of diplomatic intercourse with foreign Powers.

As regards communication with foreign Governments, it will probably be found most convenient that the Transvaal Government should correspond on such matters with Her Majesty's Government through the Resident and the High Commissioner.

There remains for consideration under this head the manner in which the relations with the independent native tribes beyond the frontier should be conducted. The general superintendence of these relations would seem naturally to fall within the functions of the British Resident under the direction of the High Commissioner. It will be for the Royal Commissioners, after examination of the whole question, to recommend what should be the precise limits of the powers assigned to the Resident in regard to this important matter. You will bear in mind that the objects to be aimed at are to preserve the peace of the frontier and to maintain a course of policy conducive generally to the interests and tranquillity of the whole of South Africa, and that Her Majesty's Government have no desire to interfere with the local administration beyond what may be indispensable for the furtherance of these objects.

A still more difficult question will be to determine what provisions shall be made for the protection of the interests of the natives who dwell within the present territorial limits of the Transvaal. The districts vary greatly in circumstances, but they may be divided into three categories:—

(1) Districts which have been really occupied by white settlement, such as Pretoria, Heidelberg, Middleburg, and Potchefstroom, where the white settlers are not much outnumbered by the natives, and where the authority of the Republican Government was thoroughly established before the annexation.

(2) Districts like Lydenburg, where the white settlements are surrounded by native tribes vastly preponderating in numbers, which either refused to recognise the rule of the Boers or give it but imperfect obedience. In the northern part of this district is Sikukuni's tribe, which we found at war with the Boers and practically independent, and which was reduced to submission by the operations of Sir Garnet Wolseley.

(3) Such districts as Zoutpansberg, where the native population is estimated at nearly 365,000 souls, whilst the white settlers are said to number only about 800, and where the authority of the Republic was at the time of the annexation scarcely acknowledged. It is true the Boers laid claim to the country and formerly held possession of parts of it, but they had been gradually pushed back by the natives, who had virtually regained their independence. The difficulty of dealing satisfactorily with the districts in the two last categories led Her Majesty's Government to think that it might be found expedient to sever from the Transvaal the eastern portion of the territory now composed within its limits, taking the Vaal River and a line drawn from the Vaal northward near the 30th degree of longitude as the new boundary. This would, however, include a part of the district of Middelburg, and it will be probably sufficient to consider the question as limited to the severance of the districts of Wakkerstroom, Utrecht, Lydenburg, and Zoutpansberg. The district of Waterberg resembles that of Zoutpansberg in the vast numerical superiority of the natives, but its position is such that it could not form a part of a separate British province, and as far as I am aware the natives had not driven back the Boer settlers in the same way as in Zoutpansberg. I will, however, refer to this district further on in connection with Zoutpansberg.

To deal first with the Wakkerstroom and Utrecht districts.

There would be one obvious advantage in retaining these

districts under British rule, inasmuch as they would separate the Transvaal State from Zululand, and prevent the recurrence of those dangerous border disputes between the Boers and the Zulus which were in large measure the cause of the Zulu war. Moreover, the existence of another authority on the Zulu border would render it extremely difficult for the British Government to maintain that influence with the Zulu Chiefs which is essential for the maintenance of peace in Zululand, and for the success of the settlement of that country made by Sir Garnet Wolseley.

The same reasons apply to that part of Lydenburg known as New Scotland, by retaining which as British the Swazis would in great measure be kept apart from the Boer frontier. If strong objections were raised on the part of the Boers to the severance from the Transvaal of the whole of Wakkerstroom, so much only might be retained as would be necessary to maintain the communications between Natal and the British territory further northward, but the Vaal River would form the most natural and convenient boundary.

With regard to the Lydenburg district apart from New Scotland, the arguments in favour of maintaining British rule over it are that the population is stated to contain an increasing British element principally at the Gold Fields, that the native population vastly outnumber the white inhabitants, being estimated at 123,300 as compared with 1578, and that having subdued Sikukuni's tribe, which occupies an important part of the district, we are under peculiar obligations to make provision for its fair treatment.

On the other hand, the Lydenburg district could scarcely be annexed to Natal, and as a separate British Province it would form an inconvenient narrow strip of territory, which would probably for some time to come not pay its own expenses. *Lastly, Her Majesty's Government are averse, on general grounds of policy, to the extension of British territory in South Africa.*

A most important consideration will be the wishes of the settlers themselves, and you will be careful to ascertain in the fullest manner whether they would willingly accept the continuance of British rule, if it should be determined to retain any of the territory to which I have referred.

O

If Sikukuni's country is not retained under British rule or declared to be an independent native district, it might be advisable that some special conditions should be made as to its relations with the Transvaal State, and should it be ultimately decided that no territory should intervene between the Transvaal State and Zululand or Swaziland, it will be necessary that the Transvaal Government should distinctly recognise the boundaries of Zululand and Swaziland as lately defined, and the independence of the latter, over whom the Republic appears to have claimed an undefined supremacy before the annexation, though it was not acknowledged by the Swazis.

I now pass to Zoutpansberg. I incline to the opinion that the most satisfactory arrangement as to this district would be that it should be left to the native tribes.

I should be glad if some similar arrangement could have been made as to Waterberg, but the reasons for leaving the district to the native tribes do not appear to be so strong as in the case of Zoutpansberg, and as the Boers have been informed that it was not the intention of Her Majesty's Government that territory should be severed from the Transvaal, west of the 30th degree of longitude, the question does not stand on the same footing.

It should be remembered, however, that the severance of the districts principally inhabited by natives would have the effect of lessening the necessity for interference for the protection of the natives within the territories of the Transvaal State, and such a measure might, therefore, recommend itself to the Boers as diminishing the occasion for action on the part of the British Government with regard to their internal affairs. It is on every account desirable that interference in those affairs should be confined to the fewest possible points, and those points should be clearly defined and embodied in the final settlement amongst the conditions upon which the Government of the country is handed over. The subject is one especially requiring examination on the spot, but I may mention one or two points as indicating the nature of the provisions which might be made, as for example, the stipulations that no law should be enacted forbidding the natives to hold land, and that they should be allowed to move as freely within the country as may be consistent with the requirements of public order, and to leave it for the purpose of seeking employment elsewhere.

The provision in the Sand River Convention against slavery, in any form, must be re-affirmed. Perhaps on some matters of especial importance affecting the natives it might be provided that the suzerain Power should have a veto upon any new legislation. Whatever provisions are made, it would be one of the duties of the British Resident to report to the High Commissioner as to their working and observance.

It is scarcely to be hoped that political passions will immediately calm down, and Her Majesty's Government are bound to take care that those who have been faithful to the British cause during the late war shall not suffer any detriment in consequence of their loyalty. Her Majesty's Government have agreed to a complete amnesty to those who have taken part with the Boers, and the Boers, on their side, have engaged that no one shall suffer molestation on account of his political opinions. It will be your duty to lay down full and explicit conditions for securing to those who have been loyal to Her Majesty, whether of English or Dutch origin, full liberty to reside in the country, with enjoyment of all civil rights and protection for their persons and property.

You will make every effort to bring to justice those who are accused of the murder of Captain Elliot, and Mr. Barber, or of any similar acts, and you will call on the Boer leaders, in accordance with their engagement to Sir Evelyn Wood, to afford you their assistance in tracing out and arresting the offenders.

Having thus gone through the principal points arising out of the agreement between Sir E. Wood and the Boers, I will proceed to notice the other matters to which I have referred.

You will find the question of the territory known as the "Keate Award" somewhat fully discussed in my Despatch of the 27th May last,* to the late Sir G. Pomeroy Colley. It was my intention on receiving his report to instruct him to determine such a new boundary as might in present circumstances appear to be the fairest to all parties, and best calculated to preserve the peace on the western frontier of

* No. 5 of [C. 2586] June 1880.

the Transvaal. Sir G. Colley had unfortunately not made any official report of the result of his visit to this territory, but I have reason to believe that he was of opinion that it was out of the question now to maintain the line laid down in 1871, by Lieutenant-Governor Keate, and that he would have recommended a new line, leaving a considerable part of the territory to the Transvaal. It will be for you to consider what line should be adopted, and you will, I have no doubt, derive valuable information and assistance from Lieut.-Colonel Moysey, R.E., the Special Commissioner in the Keate Award district. It may be found desirable to annex some part of this territory to Griqualand West or to the Orange Free State, but this must depend upon considerations which I am unable from want of local knowledge fully to appreciate. I will only add that this border has been so long in an unsettled condition that it is urgently necessary that the frontier line should be definitely fixed with as little delay as possible.

On reference to the constitution of the former South African Republic I find that there are articles which appear to infringe upon the principle of religious toleration. I am not aware that any actual impediment was placed by the State in the way of the free exercise of their religion by persons not belonging to the Dutch Reformed Church; but to prevent any misconception on the point it will be well to provide for the unrestricted exercise of their religion by all denominations within the future Transvaal State.

The Commission will have to consider the arrangements to be made for the assumption by the Transvaal State of the debt incurred in connection with the administration of the affairs of the country, whether by the South African Republic before the annexation, or by the Provincial Government subsequently.

I may refer you on this point to the declaration made by the Boer leaders in their proclamation of the 16th December last,* that the "lawful expenditure lawfully incurred for the necessary expenses of the country by the intermediate Government will be acknowledged."

There will also be other financial arrangements to be con-

* Paragraph 35, page 8 of [C. 2794] February 1880.

sidered in connection with the transfer of responsiblities and liabilities to the future Transvaal State, including such provision as is usually made on these occasions, for compensating any permanent officers displaced by the change of government.

I need scarcely say that it will be expected that full security for the continued enjoyments of their rights shall be guaranteed to all holders of property in the Transvaal, after the establishment of the new Government. I cannot doubt that the necessary undertaking will be readily given, and it will be for the Commission to consider and recommend the terms in which such undertaking should be framed. Provisions will also be required for securing to British subjects complete freedom of trade to and through the Transvaal, on the same footing as citizens of the Transvaal State. I shall transmit to you a copy of a treaty now in force, which will be of use to the Commission in considering the stipulations to be entered into on this subject.

With regard to the formal style and designation of the future Transvaal State, I am disposed to think that instead of reviving the name " South African Republic " (which never was appropriate, having regard to the fact that there were two Republics in South Africa) it would be preferable to adopt the name " Transvaal State." Before the annexation the country was very commonly spoken of as the Transvaal, and it would be convenient, as in the case of the Orange Free State, to describe it by the river which forms its southern boundary.

I shall from time to time address to you instructions upon any further point which may arise.

I have, &c.,

(Signed)   KIMBERLEY.

Sir HERCULES ROBINSON.

TELEGRAM *from* Sir H. ROBINSON, *Newcastle, to the* EARL OF KIMBERLEY.

May 22nd, 1881, Eastern Boundary.—We have fully discussed the question relating to the Eastern Boundary with the Boer leaders, and they think that the great majority of the settlers will not willingly accept the continuance of British rule over any part of the Transvaal. The leaders say that at Langs Nek they consented to leave the question to a Commission for the sake of peace and in the full confidence that we should not find it necessary to retain any part of the territory. They aver that they do not recede from their agreement, but they anticipate difficulty in securing the acquiescence of the people and think that if a retention of territory is insisted on it will leave a rankling sore behind. In their evidence, and in a letter which they have laid before us, they deprecate the retention of any part of the country by us on the grounds that it would be unjust, opposed to their interests, distasteful to their national feelings, and unnecessary from our point of view, inasmuch as a British Resident possessing comprehensive powers would, in their opinion, be able efficiently to protect native interests within the country as well as upon the frontiers. Sir E. Wood entirely dissents from this view, and is of opinion that we should at all risks retain at least the country south of the Drakensberg range for the reasons which he will explain to you in a separate message. Sir H. de Villiers and I think that there is now no course free from objection, and that we can only choose that which presents the fewest disadvantages. If we give back the whole of the country the troubles which Sir E. Wood anticipates may arise, but if we retain any part of it we think that we shall have a half rebellious white population in the part retained and a dissatisfied Transvaal State alongside. We think that under these circumstances the evils of retaining a part will be greater than the risks of giving up the whole, and we think that the latter may perhaps be lessened by conferring stringent powers upon the British Resident and giving an ultimate appeal on frontier disputes to Her Majesty's Government, whose decision in such cases the Boer leaders acknowledge is to be final. Sir H. de Villiers and I are of opinion also that the giving up of the whole country would facilitate the settlement of the other questions which have been referred to the Commission, and that the chances of the successful operation of such settlement would be increased by the prevention of future agitation. President Brand concurs in this view and tells me he is convinced that further trouble is inevitable should any part of the country be retained by us. It will now be for you to decide the line we should adopt, and, since further negotiations turn on this point, an early decision is necessary. If you agree with Sir E. Wood's view the maintenance of a considerable force in the country will be imperative for some time to come, assuming that an arrangement upon such a basis can be made at all, which we think very doubtful. If you concur in giving up the whole Sir H. de Villiers and I are of opinion that the concession should be conditional upon the powers of the British Resident being made such as we may consider it necessary to assign to him.

TELEGRAM *from* Sir EVELYN WOOD *to the*
EARL OF KIMBERLEY.

May 22, 1881.—Sir Hercules Robinson's telegram of to-day. I dissent believing the balance of disadvantages is on the other side, and that we have carried concession to the utmost limit compatible with future peace.

My telegram of 14th March expressing my view of boundary, was not approved, and the present recommendation is a compromise for the existing situation. The Resident, whatever powers are given to him, will not be able to stop native reprisals for Boer trespasses, which from need of pasturage in winter are inevitable, and I am convinced we should at all risks, so long as the Imperial Government has any responsibility here, retain at least the country south of Komati River, and on the eastern watershed of the Drakensberg. This would involve separation from the Transvaal of about six thousand square miles out of about forty thousand contained outside the line mentioned in your telegram of 17th March. The policy of that telegram was fully understood by the Boers when making peace, and they admit I informed them that I, for my part, would do my best to prevent their ruling territory adjoining large native tribes. I do not share the fear of strenuous opposition from the Boers in the district concerned, and I believe leaders now purposely exaggerate the vehemence of their followers. The Swazi king reports the resisted pressure put upon him by the Boer leaders to rise against us during the war. Under your instructions of 25th March I informed all natives that the Royal Commission would have the settlement of what land east of the 30th degree was to be retained. I believe complete withdrawal will affect pre- judicially our moral power over all natives in south-east Africa.

The Zulu war of two years ago was caused mainly by the inability of the Boers to control their frontier affairs. Their separation now from the Zulus is essential for the prevention of intrigues which will be fatal to the tranquillity of the Zulus, and to the safety of Natal. As regards the military question, I address the War Secretary.

TELEGRAM *from the* EARL OF KIMBERLEY *to* Sir H. ROBINSON, *Newcastle.*

May 30, 1881.—We have given careful consideration to telegrams of the 22nd and 23rd from you and Wood, as to Transvaal boundary, and we agree with you and Sir H. de Villiers that, for the reasons stated in your telegram, no part of the Transvaal should be retained as British territory against the will of the Boers; powers being reserved to British Government as you propose, with respect to frontier disputes ; and it being a condition that Boers fully recognise the independence of the Swazis, and the boundaries of Swaziland and Zululand, as lately defined under the authority of Her Majesty's Government.

Blue Book, C 3114, *February* 1882.

CONVENTION, 1881.

HER Majesty's Commissioners for the settlement of the Transvaal Territory, duly appointed as such by a Commission passed under the Royal Sign Manual and Signet, bearing date 5th of April 1881, do hereby undertake and guarantee on behalf of Her Majesty that from and after the 8th day of August 1881, omplete self-government, subject to the Suzerainty of Her

Majesty, her heirs and successors, will be accorded to the inhabitants of the Transvaal territory, upon the following terms and conditions, and subject to the following reservations and limitations :—

ARTICLE I.—The said Territory, to be hereinafter called the Transvaal State, will embrace the land lying between the following boundaries, to wit :

Beginning from the point where the north-eastern boundary line of Griqualand West meets the Vaal River, up the course of the Vaal River to the point of junction with it of the Klip River ; thence up the course of the Klip River to the point of junction with it of the stream called Gansvlei ; thence up the Gansvlei stream to its source in the Drakensberg ; thence to a beacon in the boundary of Natal, situated immediately opposite and close to the source of the Gansvlei stream ; thence in a north-easterly direction along the ridge of the Drakensoerg, dividing the waters flowing into the Gansvlei stream from the waters flowing into the sources of the Buffalo, to a beacon on a point where this mountain ceases to be a continuous chain ; thence to a beacon on a plain to the north-east of the last described beacon ; thence to the nearest source of a small stream called " Division Stream " ; thence down this division stream, which forms the southern boundary of the farm Sandfontein, the property of Messrs. Meek, to its junction with the Coldstream ; thence down the Coldstream to its junction with the Buffalo or Umzinyati River ; thence down the course of the Buffalo River to the junction with it of the Blood River ; thence up the course of the Blood River to the junction with it of Lyn Spruit or Dudusi ; thence up the Dudusi to its source ; thence 80 yards to Bea. I., situated on a spur of the N'Qaba-Ka-hawana Mountains ; thence 80 yards to the N'Sonto River ; thence down the N'Sonto River to its junction with the White Umvulozi River ; thence up the White Umvulozi River to a white rock where it rises ; thence 800 yards to Kambula Hill (Bea. II.) ; thence to the source of the Pemvana River, where the road from Kambula Camp to Burgers' Lager crosses ; thence down the Pemvana River to its junction with the Bivana River ; thence down the Bivana River to its junction with the Fongolo River ; thence down the Pongolo River to where it passes through the Libombo

Range; thence along the summits of the Libombo Range to the northern point of the N'Yawos Hill in that range (Bea. XVI.); thence to the northern peak of the Inkwakweni Hills (Bea. XV.); thence to Sefunda, a rocky knoll detached from and to the north-east end of the White Koppies, and to the south of the Muzana River (Bea. XIV.); thence to a point on the slope near the crest of Matanjeni, which is the name given to the south-eastern portion of the Mahamba Hills (Bea. XIII.); thence to the N'gwangwana, a double-pointed hill (one point is bare, the other wooded, the beacon being on the former), on the left bank of the Assegai River and upstream of the Dadusa Spruit (Bea. XII.); thence to the southern point of Bendita, a rocky knoll in a plain between the Little Hlozane and Assegai Rivers (Bea. XI.); thence to the highest point of Suluka Hill, round the eastern slopes of which flows the Little Hlozane, also called Ludaka or Mudspruit (Bea. X.); thence to the beacon known as "Viljoen's," or N'Duko Hill; thence to a point north-east of Derby House, known as Magwazidili's Beacon; thence to the Igaba, a small knoll on the Ungwempisi River, also called "Joubert's Beacon," and known to the natives as "Piet's Beacon" (Bea. IX.); thence to the highest point of the N'Dhlovudwalili or Houtbosch, a hill on the northern bank of the Ungwempisi River (Bea. VIII.); thence to a beacon on the only flat-topped rock, about 10 feet high, and about 30 yards in circumference at its base, situated on the south side of the Lamsamane range of hills, and overlooking the valley of the great Usuto River; this rock being 45 yards north of the road from Camden and Lake Banagher to the forests on the Usuto River (sometimes called Sandhlanas Beacon) (Bea. VII.); thence to the Gulungwana or Ibubulundi, four smooth bare hills, the highest in that neighbourhood, situated to the south of the Umtuli River (Bea. VI.); thence to a flat-topped rock, eight feet high, on the crest of the Busuku, a low rocky range south-west of the Impulazi River (Bea. V.); thence to a low bare hill on the north-east of, and overlooking the Impulazi River, to the south of it being a tributary of the Impulazi, with a considerable waterfall, and the road from the river passing 200 yards to the north-west of the beacon (Bea. IV.); thence to the highest point of the Mapumula range, the watershed of the Little Usutu River on the north, and the Umpulazi River on the south, the hill, the top of which is a bare rock, falling abruptly towards the Little Usuto (Bea. III.); thence to the western point of a double-pointed rocky hill, precipitous on all sides, called Makwana, its top being a bare rock (Bea. II.); thence to the top of a rugged hill of considerable height, falling abruptly to the Komati River, this hill being the northern extremity of the Isilotwani range, and separated from the highest peak of the ranke Inkomokasi (a sharp cone) by a deep neck (Bea. I.). (On a ridge in the straight line between Beacons I. and II. is an intermediate beacon.) From Beacon I. the boundary runs to a hill across the Komati River, and thence along the crest of the range of hills known as the Makongwa, which ruus north-east and south-west, to Kamhlubana Peak; thence in a straight line to Mananga, a point in the Libombo range, and thence to the nearest point in the Portuguese frontier on the Libombo range; thence along the summits of the Libombo range to the middle of the poort where the Komati River passes through it, called the lowest Komati Poort; thence in a north by easterly direction to Pokioens Kop, situated on the north side of the Olifant's River, where it passes through the ridges; thence about north-north-west to the nearest point of Serra di Chicundo; and thence to the junction of the Pafuri River with the Limpopo or Crocodile River: thence up the course of the Limpopo River to the point where the Marique River falls into it. Thence up the course of the Marique River to " Derde Poort," where it passes through a low range of hills, called Sikwane, a beacon (No. 10) being erected on the spur of said range near to, and westward of, the banks of the river; thence, in a straight line, through this beacon to a beacon (No. 9) erected on the top of the same range, about 1700 yards distant from beacon No. 10; thence, in a straight line, to a beacon (No. 8) erected on the highest point of an isolated hill, called Dikgagong, or " Wildebeest Kop," situated south-eastward of, and about 3⅓ miles distance from a high hill, called Moripe; thence, in a straight line, to a beacon (No. 7) erected on the summit of an isolated hill or " koppie," forming the eastern extremity of the range of hills called Moshweu, situated to the northward of, and about two miles

distant from, a large isolated hill, called Chukudu-Chochwa;
thence, in a straight line, to a beacon (No. 6) erected on the
summit of a hill, forming part of the same range, Moshwen;
thence, in a straight line, to a beacon (No. 5) erected on the
summit of a pointed hill in the same range; thence, in a
straight line, to a beacon (No. 4) erected on the summit of the
western extremity of the same range; thence, in a straight
line, to a beacon (No. 3) erected on the summit of the
northern extremity of a low, bushy hill, or " koppie," near to
and eastward of the Notwane River; thence, in a straight
line, to the junction of the stream called Metsi-Mashwane
with the Notwane River (No. 2); thence, up the course of the
Notwane River to Sengoma, being the Poort where the river
passes through the Dwarsberg range; thence, as described in
the Award given by Lieutenant-Governor Keate, dated
October 17, 1871, by Pitlanganyane (narrow place), Deboaganka
or Schaapkuil, Sibatoul (bare place), and Maclase, to
Ramatlabama, a pool on a spruit north of the Molopo River.
From Ramatlabama the boundary shall run to the summit of
an isolated hill, called Leganka; thence, in a straight line,
passing north-east of a Native Station, near " Buurman's
Drift," on the Molopo River, to that point on the road from
Mosiega to the old drift, where a road turns out through the
Native Station to the new drift below; thence to " Buurman's
Old Drift;" thence, in a straight line, to a marked and
isolated clump of trees near to and north-west of the dwelling-
house of C. Austin, a tenant on the farm " Vleifontein,"
No. 17; thence, in a straight line, to the north-western corner
beacon of the farm " Mooimeisjesfontein," No. 30; thence,
along the western line of the said farm " Mooimeisjesfontein,"
and in prolongation thereof, as far as the road leading from
" Ludik's Drift," on the Molopo River, past the homestead of
" Mooimeisjesfontein," towards the Salt Pans near Hart
River; thence, along the said road, to a point thereon, eight
miles north of the dwelling of Gouws, at a Salt Pan; thence,
in a straight line, to a point one mile due west of the more
northerly Pan, measured from its western edge; thence, in a
straight line, to the most westerly beacon of the farm Rietpan,
No. 150; thence along the line of the said farm to the drift on
the Hart River, near the ruined house, known as " Lieben-

berg's"; thence down the Hart River to the drift about two-and-a-half miles below Mamusa and opposite the dwelling-house of Theodore Doms; thence, in a straight line, to the summit of an isolated hill, known as "Koppie Enkel," situated between the Vaal and Hart Rivers, and about 36 miles from Mamusa, and about 18 miles north of the village of Christiana; thence, in a straight line, to that point on the north-east boundary of Griqualand West as beaconed by Mr. Surveyor Ford, where two farms, registered as Nos. 72 and 75, do meet, about midway between the Vaal and Hart Rivers, measured along the said boundary of Griqualand West; thence to the first point where the north-east boundary of Griqualand West meets the Vaal River.

ARTICLE 2.—Her Majesty reserves to herself, her heirs and successors, (a) the right from time to time *to appoint a British Resident* in and for the said State, with such duties and functions as are hereinafter defined; (b) the *right to move troops* through the said State in time of war, or in case of the apprehension of immediate war between the suzerain Power and any foreign State, or Native tribe in South Africa; and (c) the control of the external relations of the said State, including the conclusion of treaties, and the conduct of diplomatic intercourse with foreign Powers, such intercourse to be carried on through Her Majesty's diplomatic and consular officers abroad.

ARTICLE 3.—Until altered by the Volksraad or other competent authority, all laws, whether passed before or after the annexation of the Transvaal Territory to Her Majesty's dominions, shall, except in so far as they are inconsistent with, or repugnant to, the provisions of this Convention, be and remain in force in the said State, in so far as they shall be applicable thereto: Provided that no future enactment specially affecting the interests of Natives shall have any force or effect in the said State without the consent of Her Majesty, her heirs and successors, first had and obtained and signified to the Government of the said State through the British Resident: Provided further, that in no case will the repeal or amendment of any laws which have been enacted since the Annexation have a retrospective effect so as to invalidate any acts done or liabilities incurred by virtue of such laws.

ARTICLE 4.—On the 8th day of August, 1881, the Government of the said State, together with all rights and obligations thereto appertaining, and all State property taken over at the time of annexation, save and except munitions of war, will be handed over to

Messrs. STEPHANUS JOHANNES PAULUS KRUGER,
MARTINUS WESSEL PRETORIUS, and
PETRUS JACOBUS JOUBERT,

or the survivor or survivors of them, who will forthwith cause a Volksraad to be elected and convened; and the Volksraad thus elected and convened will decide as to the further administration of the Government of the said State.

ARTICLE 5.—All sentences passed upon persons who may be convicted of offences contrary to the rules of civilised warfare, committed during the recent hostilities, will be duly carried out, and no alteration or mitigation of such sentences will be made or allowed by the Government of the Transvaal State without Her Majesty's consent, conveyed through the British Resident. In case there shall be any prisoners in any of the gaols of the Transvaal State, whose respective sentences of imprisonment have been remitted in part by Her Majesty's Administrator, or other officer administering the Government, such remission will be recognised and acted upon by the future Government of the said State.

ARTICLE 6.—Her Majesty's Government will make due compensation for all losses or damage sustained by reason of such acts as are in the 8th Article hereinafter specified, which may have been committed by Her Majesty's forces during the recent hostilities, except for such losses or damage as may already have been compensated for, and the Government of the Transvaal State will make due compensation for all losses or damage sustained by reason of such acts as are in the 8th Article hereinafter specified, which may have been committed by the people who were in arms against Her Majesty during the recent hostilities, except for such losses or damage as may already have been compensated for.

ARTICLE 7.—The decision of all claims for compensation, as in the last preceding article mentioned, will be referred to a sub-commission, consisting of the Honourable George Hudson, the Honourable Jacobus Petrus de Wet, and the Honourable John Gilbert Kotzé.

In case one or more of such Sub-Commissioners shall be unable or unwilling to act, the remaining Sub-Commissioner or Sub-Commissioners will, after consultation with the Government of the Transvaal State, submit for the approval of Her Majesty's High Commissioner, the names of one or more persons to be appointed by him, to fill the place or places thus vacated.

The decision of the said Sub-Commissioners, or of a majority of them, will be final.

The said Sub-Commissioners will enter upon and perform their duties with all convenient speed. They will, before taking evidence, or ordering evidence to be taken, in respect of any claim, decide whether such claim can be entertained at all under the rules laid down in the next succeeding article.

In regard to claims which can be so entertained, the Sub-Commissioners will, in the first instance, afford every facility for an amicable arrangement as to the amount payable in respect of any claim, and only in cases in which there is no reasonable ground for believing that an immediate amicable arrangement can be arrived at, will they take evidence, or order evidence to be taken.

For the purpose of taking evidence and reporting thereon, the Sub-Commissioners may appoint deputies, who will without delay submit records of the evidence and their reports to the Sub-Commissioners.

The Sub-Commissioners will arrange their sittings, and the sittings of their deputies, in such a manner as to afford the greatest convenience to the parties concerned and their witnesses. In no case will costs be allowed to either side, other than the actual and reasonable expenses of witnesses whose evidence is certified by the Sub-Commissioners to have been necessary. Interest will not run on the amount of any claim except as hereinafter provided for.

The said Sub-Commissioners will forthwith, after deciding upon any claim, announce their decision to the Government against which the award is made, and to the claimant.

The amount of remuneration payable to the Sub-Commissioners and their deputies will be determined by the High

Commissioner after all the claims have been decided upon.
The British Government and the Government of the Transvaal
State will pay proportionate shares of the said remuneration,
and of the expenses of the Sub-Commissioners and their
deputies, according to the amounts awarded against them
respectively.

ARTICLE 8.—For the purpose of distinguishing claims to be
accepted from those to be rejected the Sub-Commissioners
will be guided by the following rules, viz. :—Compensation
will be allowed for losses or damage sustained by reason of
the following acts committed during the recent hostilities,
viz. :—(a) commandeering, seizure, confiscation, or destruction
of property, or damage done to property ; (b) violence done
or threats used by persons in arms.

In regard to acts under (a), compensation will be allowed
for direct losses only.

In regard to acts falling under (b), compensation will be
allowed for actual losses of property, or actual injury to the
same, proved to have been caused by its enforced abandonment.

No claims for indirect losses, except such as are in this
Article specially provided for, will be entertained.

No claims which have been handed in to the Secretary of
the Royal Commission after the 1st day of July 1881, will be
entertained, unless the Sub-Commissioners shall be satisfied
that the delay was reasonable.

When claims for loss of property are considered, the Sub-
Commissioners will require distinct proof of the existence of
the property, and that it neither has reverted, nor will revert,
to the claimant.

ARTICLE 9.—The Government of the Transvaal State will
pay and satisfy the amount of every claim awarded against it
within one month after the Sub-Commissioners shall have
notified their decision to the said Government, and in default
of such payment the said Government will pay interest at the
rate of six per cent. per annum from the date of such default ;
but Her Majesty's Government may, at any time before such
payment, pay the amount, with interest, if any, to the claimant
in satisfaction of his claim, and may add the sum thus paid
to any debt which may be due by the Transvaal State to Her
Majesty's Government, as hereinafter provided for.

ARTICLE 10.—The Transvaal State will be liable for the balance of the debts for which the South African Republic was liable at the date of annexation, to wit: the sum of £48,000 in respect of the Cape Commercial Bank Loan, and £85,667 in respect of the Railway Loan, together with the amount due on 8th August 1881, on account of the Orphan Chamber debt which now stands at £27,226 15s., which debts will be a first charge upon the revenues of the State. The Transvaal State will moreover be liable for the lawful expenditure lawfully incurred for the necessary expenses of the Province since annexation, to wit: the sum of £265,000, which debt, together with such debts as may be incurred by virtue of the 9th Article, will be a second charge upon the revenues of the State.

ARTICLE 11.—The debts due as aforesaid by the Transvaal State to Her Majesty's Government will bear interest at the rate of three and a half per cent., and any portion of such debt as may remain unpaid on 8th August, 1882, shall be repayable by a payment for interest and sinking fund of six pounds and ninepence per £100 per annum, which will extinguish the debt in twenty-five years. The said payment of six pounds and ninepence per £100 shall be payable half-yearly, in British currency, on the 8th February and 8th August in each year: provided always that the Transvaal State shall pay, in reduction of the said debt the sum of £100,000 before 8th August, 1882, and shall be at liberty at the close of any half-year to pay off the whole or any portion of the outstanding debt.

ARTICLE 12.—All persons holding property in the said State on the 8th day of August, 1881, will continue to enjoy the rights of property which they have enjoyed since the annexation. No person who has remained loyal to Her Majesty during the recent hostilities shall suffer any molestation by reason of his loyalty; or be liable to any criminal prosecution or civil action for any part taken in connection with such hostilities; and all such persons will have full liberty to reside in the country, with enjoyment of all civil rights, and protection for their persons and property.

ARTICLE 13.—Natives will be allowed to acquire land, but the grant or transfer of such land will in every case be made to and registered in the name of the Native Location Commission herein-after mentioned, in trust for such natives.

ARTICLE 14.—Natives will be allowed to move as freely within the country as may be consistent with the requirements of public order, and to leave it for the purpose of seeking employment elsewhere, or for other lawful purposes, subject always to the Pass Laws of the said State, as amended by the Legislature of the Province, or as may hereafter be enacted, under the provisions of the 3rd Article of this Convention.

ARTICLE 15.—The provisions of the 4th Article of the Sand River Convention are hereby re-affirmed, and no slavery or apprenticeship partaking of slavery will be tolerated by the Government of the said State.

ARTICLE 16.—There will continue to be complete freedom of religion and protection from molestation for all denominations, provided the same be not inconsistent with morality and good order; and no disability shall attach to any person in regard to rights of property by reason of the religious opinions which he holds.

ARTICLE 17.—The British Resident will receive from the Government of the Transvaal State such assistance and support as can by law be given to him for the due discharge of his functions. He will also receive every assistance for the proper care and preservation of the graves of such of Her Majesty's forces as have died in the Transvaal ; and, if need be, for the expropriation of land for the purpose.

ARTICLE 18.—The following will be the duties and functions of the British Resident :—

(1) He will perform duties and functions analogous to those discharged by a Chargé d'Affaires and Consul General.

(2) In regard to natives within the Transvaal State he will, (a) report to the High Commissioner, as representative of the Suzerain, as to the working and observance of the provisions of this Convention ; (b) report to the Transvaal authorities any cases of ill-treatment of natives, or attempts to incite natives to rebellion, that may come to his knowledge ; (c) use his influence with the natives in favour of law and order ; and

(*d*) generally perform such other duties as are by this Convention entrusted to him, and take such steps for the protection of the persons and property of natives as are consistent with the laws of the land.

(3) In regard to natives not residing in the Transvaal, (*a*) he will report to the High Commissioner and the Transvaal Government any encroachments reported to him as having been made by Transvaal residents upon the land of such natives, and in case of disagreement between the Transvaal Government and the British Resident, as to whether an encroachment had been made, the decision of the Suzerain will be final. (*b*) The British Resident will be the medium of communication with native chiefs outside the Transvaal, and, subject to the approval of the High Commissioner, as representing the suzerain, he will control the conclusion of treaties with them, and (*c*) he will arbitrate upon every dispute between Transvaal residents and natives outside the Transvaal (as to acts committed beyond the boundaries of the Transvaal) which may be referred to him by the parties interested.

(4) In regard to communications with foreign Powers, the Transvaal Government will correspond with Her Majesty's Government through the British Resident and the High Commissioner.

ARTICLE 19.—The Government of the Transvaal State will strictly adhere to the boundaries defined in the first Article of this Convention, and will do its utmost to prevent any of its inhabitants from making any encroachment upon lands beyond the said State. The Royal Commission will forthwith appoint a person who will beacon off the boundary line between Ramatlabama and the point where such line first touches the Griqualand West boundary, midway between the Vaal and Hart rivers. The person so appointed will be instructed to make an arrangement between the owners of the farms "Grootfontein" and "Vallefontein" on the one hand and the Barolong authorities on the other, by which a fair share of the water supply of the said farms shall be allowed to flow undisturbed to the said Barolongs.

ARTICLE 20.—All grants or titles issued at any time by the Transvaal Government in respect of land outside the boundary of the Transvaal State, as defined in Article 1, shall be considered invalid and of no effect, except in so far as any such grant or title relates to land that falls within the boundary of the Transvaal State; and all persons holding any such grant so considered invalid and of no effect will receive from the Government of the Transvaal State such compensation, either in land or in money, as the Volksraad shall determine. In all cases in which any native chiefs or other authorities outside the said boundaries have received any adequate consideration from the Government of the former South African Republic for land excluded from the Transvaal by the first Article of this Convention, or where permanent improvements have been made on the land, the British Resident will, subject to the approval of the High Commissioner, use his influence to recover from the native authorities fair compensation for the loss of the land thus excluded, or of the permanent improvements thereon.

ARTICLE 21.—Forthwith, after the taking effect of this Convention, a Native Location Commission will be constituted, consisting of the President (or in his absence the Vice-President) of the State, or some one deputed by him, the Resident, or some one deputed by him, and a third person to be agreed upon by the President (or the Vice-President, as the case may be) and the Resident; and such Commission will be a standing body for the performance of the duties herein-after mentioned.

ARTICLE 22.—The Native Location Commission will reserve to the native tribes of the State such locations as they may be fairly and equitably entitled to, due regard being had to the actual occupation of such tribes. The Native Location Commission will clearly define the boundaries of such locations, and for that purpose will, in every instance, first of all ascertain the wishes of the parties interested in such land. In case land already granted in individual titles shall be required for the purpose of any location, the owners will receive such compensation, either in other land or in money, as the Volksraad shall determine. After the boundaries of any location have been fixed, no fresh grant of land within such location will be made, nor will the boundaries be altered without the consent of the Location Commission. No fresh grants of land will be made in the districts of Waterberg, Zoutpansberg, and Lydenburg, until the locations in the said districts respectively shall have been defined by the said Commission.

ARTICLE 23.—If not released before the taking effect of this Convention, Sikukuni, and those of his followers who have been imprisoned with him, will be forthwith released, and the boundaries of his location will be defined by the Native Location Commission in the manner indicated in the last preceding Article.

ARTICLE 24.—The independence of the Swazis, within the boundary line of Swaziland, as indicated in the first article of this Convention, will be fully recognised.

ARTICLE 25.—No other or higher duties will be imposed on the importation into the Transvaal State of any article, the produce or manufacture of the dominions and possessions of Her Majesty, from whatever place arriving, than are or may be payable on the like article, the produce or manufacture of any other country, nor will any prohibition be maintained or imposed on the importation of any article, the produce or manufacture of the dominions and possessions of Her Majesty, which shall not equally extend to the importation of the like articles, being the produce or manufacture of any other country.

ARTICLE 26.—All persons other than Natives conforming themselves to the laws of the Transvaal State (a) will have full liberty, with their families, to enter, travel, or reside in any part of the Transvaal State; (b) they will be entitled to hire or possess houses, manufactories, warehouses, shops, and premises; (c) they may carry on their commerce either in person or by any agents whom they may think fit to employ: (d) they will not be subject, in respect to their persons or property, or in respect to their commerce or industry, to any taxes, whether general or local, other than those which are or may be imposed upon Transvaal citizens.

ARTICLE 27.—All inhabitants of the Transvaal shall have free access to the Courts of Justice for the prosecution and defence of their rights.

ARTICLE 28.—All persons, other than natives, who estab-lished their domicile in the Transvaal between the 12th day of April 1877 and the date when this convention comes into effect, and who shall within 12 months after such last-mentioned date have their names registered by the British Resident, shall be exempt from all compulsory military service whatever. The Resident shall notify such registration to the Government of the Transvaal State.

ARTICLE 29. — Provision shall hereafter be made by a separate instrument for the mutual extradition of criminals, and also for the surrender of deserters from Her Majesty's forces.

ARTICLE 30.—All debts contracted since the annexation will be payable in the same currency in which they may have been contracted.

All uncancelled postage and other revenue stamps issued by the Government since the annexation will remain valid, and will be accepted at their present value by the future Government of the State. All licences duly issued since the annexation will remain in force during the period for which they may have been issued.

ARTICLE 31.—No grants of land which may have been made, and no transfers or mortgages which may have been passed since the date of annexation, will be invalidated by reason merely of their having been made or passed after such date.

All transfers to the British Secretary for Native Affairs in trust for natives will remain in force, the Native Location Commission taking the place of such Secretary for Native Affairs.

ARTICLE 32.—This Convention will be ratified by a newly elected Volksraad within the period of three months after its execution, and in default of such ratification this convention shall be null and void.

ARTICLE 33. — Forthwith after the ratification of this Convention, as in the last preceding article mentioned, all British troops in Transvaal territory will leave the same, and the mutual delivery of munitions of war will be carried out.

Signed at Pretoria, this 3rd day of August, 1881.

HERCULES ROBINSON,
President and High Commissioner.
EVELYN WOOD, MAJOR-GENERAL,
Officer Administering the Government.
J. H. DE VILLIERS.

Royal Commissioners.

We, the undersigned, Stephanus Johannes Paulus Kruger, Martinus Wessel Pretorius, and Petrus Jacobus Joubert, as representatives of the Transvaal Burghers, do hereby agree to all the above conditions, reservations, and limitations, under which self-government has been restored to the inhabitants of the Transvaal territory, subject to the suzerainty of Her Majesty, her heirs and successors, and we agree to accept the Government of the said territory, with all rights and obligations thereto appertaining, on the 8th day of August, 1881, and we promise and undertake that this convention shall be ratified by a newly elected Volksraad of the Transvaal State within three months from this date.

Signed at Pretoria, this 3rd day of August, 1881.

S. J. P. KRUGER.
M. W. PRETORIUS.
P. J. JOUBERT.

Blue Book, C 3914, 1884.

A CONVENTION *between* HER MAJESTY THE QUEEN *of the United Kingdom of Great Britain and Ireland and the South African Republic.*

Whereas the Government of the Transvaal State, through its Delegates, consisting of Stephanus Johannes Paulus Kruger, President of the said State, Stephanus Jacobus Du Toit, Superintendent of Education, and Nicholas Jacobus Smit, a member of the Volksraad, have represented that the Convention signed at Pretoria on the 3rd day of August 1881, and ratified by the Volksraad of the said State on the 25th October 1881, contains certain provisions which are inconvenient, and imposes burdens and obligations from which the said State is desirous to be relieved, and that the south-western boundaries fixed by the said Convention should be amended, with a view to promote the peace and good order of the said State, and of the countries adjacent thereto; and whereas Her Majesty the Queen of the United Kingdom of Great Britain and Ireland has been pleased to take the said representations into consideration. Now, therefore, Her Majesty has been pleased to direct, and it is hereby declared, that the following Articles of a new Convention, signed on behalf of Her Majesty by Her Majesty's High Commissioner in South Africa, the Right Honourable Sir Hercules George Robert Robinson, Knight Grand Cross of the Most Distinguished order of Saint Michael and Saint George, Governor of the Colony of the Cape of Good Hope, and on behalf of the Transvaal State (which shall herein-after be called the South African Republic) by the above-named Delegates, Stephanus Johannes Paulus Kruger, Stephanus Jacobus Du Toit, and Nicholas Jacobus Smit, shall, when ratified by the Volksraad of the South African Republic, be substituted for the articles embodied in the Convention of 3rd August 1881; which latter, pending such ratification, shall continue in full force and effect.

ARTICLES.

ARTICLE 1.—The Territory of the South African Republic will embrace the land lying between the following boundaries, to wit:*

ARTICLE 2.—The Government of the South African Republic will strictly adhere to the boundaries defined in the first Article of this Convention, and will do its utmost to prevent any of its inhabitants from making any encroachments upon lands beyond the said boundaries. The Government of the South African Republic will appoint Commissioners upon the eastern and western borders whose duty it will be strictly to

* These boundaries are almost identical with those specified in the Convention of 1881, and therefore are not reproduced.

guard against irregularities and all trespassing over the boundaries. Her Majesty's Government will, if necessary, appoint
Commissioners in the native territories outside the eastern
and western borders of the South African Republic to maintain
order and prevent encroachments.

Her Majesty's Government and the Government of the
South African Republic will each appoint a person to proceed
together to beacon off the amended south-west boundary as
described in Article 1 of this Convention; and the President
of the Orange Free State shall be requested to appoint a
referee to whom the said persons shall refer any questions on
which they may disagree respecting the interpretation of the
said Article, and the decision of such referee thereon shall be
final. The arrangement already made, under the terms of
Article 19 of the Convention of Pretoria of the 3rd August
1881, between the owners of the farms Grootfontein and Vallei-
fontein on the one hand, and the Barolong authorities on the
other, by which a fair share of the water supply of the said
farms shall be allowed to flow undisturbed to the said Barolongs, shall continue in force.

ARTICLE 3.—If a British officer is appointed to reside at
Pretoria or elsewhere within the South African Republic to
discharge functions analogous to those of a Consular officer
he will receive the protection and assistance of the Republic.

ARTICLE 4.—The South African Republic will conclude no
treaty or engagement with any State or nation other than the
Orange Free State, nor with any native tribe to the eastward
or westward of the Republic, until the same has been approved
by Her Majesty the Queen.

Such approval shall be considered to have been granted if
Her Majesty's Government shall not, within six months after
receiving a copy of such treaty (which shall be delivered to
them immediately upon its completion), have notified that the
conclusion of such treaty is in conflict with the interests of
Great Britain or of any of Her Majesty's possessions in South
Africa.

ARTICLE 5.—The South African Republic will be liable for
any balance which may still remain due of the debts for which
it was liable at the date of Annexation, to wit, the Cape
Commercial Bank Loan, the Railway Loan, and the Orphan

Chamber Debt, which debts will be a first charge upon the revenues of the Republic. The South African Republic will moreover be liable to Her Majesty's Government for £250,000, which will be a second charge upon the revenues of the Republic.

ARTICLE 6. — The debt due as aforesaid by the South African Republic to Her Majesty's Government will bear interest at the rate of three and a half per cent. from the date of the ratification of this Convention, and shall be repayable by a payment for interest and Sinking Fund of six pounds and ninepence per £100 per annum, which will extinguish the debt in twenty-five years. The said payment of six pounds and ninepence per £100 shall be payable half-yearly, in British currency, at the close of each half-year from the date of such ratification: Provided always that the South African Republic shall be at liberty at the close of any half-year to pay off the whole or any portion of the outstanding debt.

Interest at the rate of three and a half per cent. on the debt as standing under the Convention of Pretoria shall as heretofore be paid to the date of the ratification of this Convention.

ARTICLE 7. — All persons who held property in the Transvaal on the 8th day of August 1881, and still hold the same, will continue to enjoy the rights of property which they have enjoyed since the 12th April 1877. No person who has remained loyal to Her Majesty during the late hostilities shall suffer any molestation by reason of his loyalty; or be liable to any criminal prosecution or civil action for any part taken in connexion with such hostilities; and all such persons will have full liberty to reside in the country, with enjoyment of all civil rights, and protection for their persons and property.

ARTICLE 8. — The South African Republic 'renews the declaration made in the Sand River Convention, and in the Convention of Pretoria, that no slavery or apprenticeship partaking of slavery will be tolerated by the Government of the said Republic.

ARTICLE 9.—There will continue to be complete freedom of religion and protection from molestation for all denominations, provided the same be not inconsistent with morality and good order; and no disability shall attach to any person in regard to rights of property by reason of the religious opinions which he holds.

ARTICLE 10.—The British Officer appointed to reside in the South African Republic will receive every assistance from the Government of the said Republic in making due provision for the proper care and preservation of the graves of such of Her Majesty's Forces as have died in the Transvaal; and if need be, for the appropriation of land for the purpose.

ARTICLE 11.—All grants or titles issued at any time by the Transvaal Government in respect of land outside the boundary of the South African Republic, as defined in Article 1, shall be considered invalid and of no effect, except in so far as any such grant or title relates to lands that falls within the boundary of the South African Republic; and all persons holding any such grant so considered invalid and of no effect will receive from the Government of the South African Republic such compensation, either in land or in money, as the Volksraad shall determine. In all cases in which any Native Chiefs or other authorities outside the said boundaries have received any adequate consideration from the Government of the South African Republic for land excluded from the Transvaal by the first Article of this Convention, or where permanent improvements have been made on the land, the High Commissioner will recover from the native authorities fair compensation for the loss of the land thus excluded, or of the permanent improvements thereon.

ARTICLE 12.—The independence of the Swazis, within the boundary line of Swaziland, as indicated in the first Article of this Convention, will be fully recognised.

ARTICLE 13. — Except in pursuance of any treaty or engagement made as provided in Article 4 of this Convention, no other or higher duties shall be imposed on the importation into the South African Republic of any article coming from any part of Her Majesty's dominions than are or may be imposed on the like article coming from any other place or country; nor will any prohibition be maintained or imposed on the importation into the South African Republic of any part of Her Majesty's dominions which shall not equally extend to the like article coming from any other place or country. And in like manner the same treatment shall be given to any article coming to Great Britain from the South African Republic as to the like article coming from any other place or country.

These provisions do not preclude the consideration of special arrangements as to import duties and commercial relations between the South African Republic and any of Her Majesty's colonies or possessions.

ARTICLE 14.—All persons, other than 'natives, conforming themselves to the laws of the South African Republic (a) will have full liberty, with their families, to enter, travel, or reside in any part of the South African Republic ; (b) they will be entitled to hire or possess houses, manufactories, warehouses, shops, and premises ; (c) they may carry on their commerce either in person or by any agents whom they may think fit to employ; (d) they will not be subject, in respect of their persons or property, or in respect of their commerce or industry, to any taxes, whether general or local, other than those which are or may be imposed upon citizens of the said Republic.

ARTICLE 15. — All persons, other than natives, who established their domicile in the Transvaal between the 12th day of April 1877 and the 8th August 1881, and who within twelve months after such last-mentioned date have had their names registered by the British Resident, shall be exempt from all compulsory military service whatever.

ARTICLE 16.—Provision shall hereafter be made by a separate instrument for the mutual extradition of criminals, and also for the surrender of deserters from Her Majesty's Forces.

ARTICLE 17.—All debts contracted between the 12th April 1877 and the 8th August 1881 will be payable in the same currency in which they may have been contracted.

ARTICLE 18. — No grants of land which may have been made, and no transfers or mortgages which may have been passed between the 12th April 1877 and 8th August 1881, will be invalidated by reason merely of their having been made or passed between such dates.

All transfers to the British Secretary for Native Affairs in trust for natives will remain in force, an officer of the South African Republic taking the place of such Secretary for Native Affairs.

ARTICLE 19.—The Government of the South African Republic will engage faithfully to fulfil the assurances given, in accordance with the laws in the South African Republic, to the natives at the Pretoria Pitso by the Royal Commission in the presence of the Triumvirate and with their entire assent, (1) as to the freedom of the natives to buy or otherwise acquire land under certain conditions, (2) as to the appointment of a commission to mark out native locations, (3) as to the access of the natives to the courts of law, and (4) as to their being allowed to move freely within the country, or to leave it for any legal purpose, under a pass system.

ARTICLE 20.—This Convention will be ratified by a Volksraad of the South African Republic within the period of six months after its execution, and in default of such ratification this Convention shall be null and void.

Signed in duplicate in London this 27th day of February 1884.

(Signed)	HERCULES ROBINSON.
(Signed)	S. J. P. KRUGER.
(Signed)	S. J. DU TOIT.
(Signed)	M. J. SMIT.

INDEX

(The numerals refer to the page)

Printed by BALLANTYNE, HANSON & Co.
London & Edinburgh

Lightning Source UK Ltd.
Milton Keynes UK
UKHW010753211118
332624UK00007B/430/P